Lecture Notes in Computer Science 9480

Commenced Publication in 1973
Founding and Former Series Editors:
Gerhard Goos, Juris Hartmanis, and Jan van Leeuwen

More information about this series at http://www.springer.com/series/8637

Abdelkader Hameurlain · Josef Küng
Roland Wagner · Tran Khanh Dang
Nam Thoai (Eds.)

Transactions on Large-Scale Data- and Knowledge- Centered Systems XXIII

Selected Papers from FDSE 2014

Springer

Editors-in-Chief
Abdelkader Hameurlain
IRIT, Paul Sabatier University
Toulouse
France

Roland Wagner
FAW, University of Linz
Linz
Austria

Josef Küng
FAW, University of Linz
Linz
Austria

Guest Editors
Tran Khanh Dang
Ho Chi Minh City University of Technology
Ho Chi Minh City
Vietnam

Nam Thoai
Ho Chi Minh City University of Technology
Ho Chi Minh City
Vietnam

ISSN 0302-9743   ISSN 1611-3349 (electronic)
Lecture Notes in Computer Science
ISBN 978-3-662-49174-4   ISBN 978-3-662-49175-1 (eBook)
DOI 10.1007/978-3-662-49175-1

Library of Congress Control Number: 2015958557

This Springer imprint is published by SpringerNature
The registered company is Springer-Verlag GmbH Berlin Heidelberg

Preface

The First International Conference on Future Data and Security Engineering (FDSE) was held in Ho Chi Minh City, Vietnam, November 19–21, 2014. FDSE is to become an annual international forum designed for researchers and practitioners interested in state-of-the-art and state-of-the-practice activities in data, information, knowledge, and security engineering to explore cutting-edge ideas, present and exchange their research results and advanced data-intensive applications, as well as to discuss emerging issues on data, information, knowledge, and security engineering. We invited the submission of both original research contributions and industry papers. At the annual FDSE, researchers and practitioners will not only be able to share research solutions to problems of today's data and security engineering society, but also identify new issues and directions for future related research and development work.

FDSE 2014 received 66 submissions and, after a careful review process, only 23 papers were selected for presentation. Among those great papers, we selected only five papers to invite the authors to revise, extend, and resubmit for publication in this special issue. The main focus of this special issue is on advanced computing issues in information and security engineering as well as their promising applications.

The great success of FDSE 2014 as well as this special issue of TLDKS was the result of the efforts of many people, to whom we would like to express our gratitude. First, we would like to thank all authors who extended and submitted papers to this special issue. We would also like to thank the members of the committees and external reviewers for their timely reviewing and lively participation in the subsequent discussion in order to select such high-quality papers published in this issue. Finally yet importantly, we thank Gabriela Wagner for her enthusiastic help and support during the whole process of preparation for this publication.

September 2015

Tran Khanh Dang
Nam Thoai

Organization

Minh-Quang Tran   HCMC University of Technology, Vietnam and National
                                 Institute of Informatics, Japan
Hoang Tam Vo   SAP and National University of Singapore, Singapore
Nguyen Ngoc Thien An   University College Dublin, Ireland
Viet-Hung Nguyen   University of Trento, Italy
Phan Trong Nhan   Johannes Kepler University Linz, Austria
Quoc Cuong To   INRIA Rocquencourt, Versailles, France
Le Thi Kim Tuyen   Sungkyunkwan University, South Korea
Tran Tri Dang   HCMC University of Technology, Vietnam

Contents

A Natural Language Processing Tool for White Collar Crime Investigation

Maarten van Banerveld[2], Mohand-Tahar Kechadi[1],
and Nhien-An Le-Khac[1(✉)]

[1] School of Computer Science and Informatics,
University College Dublin, Belfield, Dublin 4, Ireland
{tahar.kechadi,an.lekhac}@ucd.ie
[2] Surinameweg, 42035 VA Haarlem, The Netherlands
mj.van.barneveld@belastingdienst.nl

Abstract. In today's world we are confronted with increasing amounts of information every day coming from a large variety of sources. People and corporations are producing data on a large scale, and since the rise of the internet, e-mail and social media the amount of produced data has grown exponentially. From a law enforcement perspective we have to deal with these huge amounts of data when a criminal investigation is launched against an individual or company. Relevant questions need to be answered like who committed the crime, who were involved, what happened and on what time, who were communicating and about what? Not only the amount of available data to investigate has increased enormously, but also the complexity of this data has increased. When these communication patterns need to be combined with for instance a seized financial administration or corporate document shares a complex investigation problem arises. Recently, criminal investigators face a huge challenge when evidence of a crime needs to be found in the Big Data environment where they have to deal with large and complex datasets especially in financial and fraud investigations. To tackle this problem, a financial and fraud investigation unit of a European country has developed a new tool named LES that uses Natural Language Processing (NLP) techniques to help criminal investigators handle large amounts of textual information in a more efficient and faster way. In this paper, we present this tool and we focus on the evaluation its performance in terms of the requirements of forensic investigation: speed, smarter and easier for investigators. In order to evaluate this LES tool, we use different performance metrics. We also show experimental results of our evaluation with large and complex datasets from real-world application.

Keywords: Big data · Natural language processing · Financial and fraud investigation · Hadoop/MapReduce

1 Introduction

Since the start of the digital information age to the rise of the Internet, the amount of digital data has dramatically increased. Indeed, we are dealing with many challenges when it comes to data. Some data is structured and stored in a traditional relational

© Springer-Verlag Berlin Heidelberg 2016
A. Hameurlain et al. (Eds.): TLDKS XXIII, LNCS 9480, pp. 1–22, 2016.
DOI: 10.1007/978-3-662-49175-1_1

database, while other data, including documents, customer service records, and even pictures and videos, is unstructured. Organizations also have to consider new sources of data generated by new devices such as sensors. Moreover, there are other new key data sources, such as social media, click-stream data generated from website interactions, etc. The availability and adoption of newer, more powerful mobile devices, coupled with ubiquitous access to global networks will drive the creation of more new sources for data. As a consequence, we are living in the Big Data era. Big Data can be defined as any kind of datasets that has three important characteristics: huge volumes, very high velocity and very wide variety of data. Obviously, handling and analysing large, complex, and velocity data have always offered the greatest challenges as well as benefits for organisations of all sizes. Global competitions, dynamic markets, and rapid development in the information and communication technologies are some of the major challenges in today's industry. Briefly, we have had a deluge of data from not only science fields but also industry, commerce and digital forensics fields. Although the amount of data available to us is constantly increasing, our ability to process it becomes more and more difficult. This is especially true for the criminal investigation today. For instance, a criminal investigation department CID[1] of the Customs Force in a European country has to analyse around 3.5 Terabyte of data (per case) to combat fiscal, financial-economic and commodity fraud safeguards the integrity of the financial system and to combat also organized crime, especially its financial component.

Actually, CID staff focuses on the criminal prosecution of: Fiscal fraud (including VAT/carousel fraud, excise duty fraud or undisclosed foreign assets); Financial-economic fraud (insider trading, bankruptcy fraud, property fraud, money laundering, etc.); Fraud involving specific goods (strategic goods and sanctions, raw materials for drugs, intellectual property, etc.). Seizing the business accounts is usually the first step in the investigation. The fraud must be proved by means of the business accounts (among other things). Investigation officers not only investigate paper accounts, but also digital records such as computer hard disks or information on (corporate) networks. The fraud investigation unit uses special software to investigate these digital records. In this way we gain an insight into the fraud and how it was committed. Interviewing or interrogation of a suspect is an invariable part of the investigation. A suspect can make a statement, but may also refuse this. In any case, the suspect must be given the opportunity to explain the facts of which he is suspected. During their activities the investigation officers can rely on the Information-gathering teams for information and advice. These teams gather, process and distribute relevant information and conduct analyses. With digital investigations we respond to the rapid digitalization of society. This digitalization has led to new fraud patterns and methods, and all kinds of swindle via the Internet. In order to trace these fraudsters we use the same digital possibilities as they do.

As the CID handles around 450 criminal investigations every year, the amount of (digital-) data that is collected increases year over year. A specific point of attention is that the CID operates in another spectrum of investigations as 'regular' police

---

[1] Real name of department as well as all of its customer names (banks, etc.) cannot be disclosed because of confidential agreement of the project.

departments. The types of crime that the CID needs to investigate mostly revolve around written facts. So the evidence that is collected by the CID by default contains of large amounts of textual data. One can imagine how much textual data a multinational firm produces, and how many e-mails are being sent in such companies. A specific challenge for law enforcement departments that are involved with fraud investigations is: how can we find the evidence we need in these huge amounts of complex data. Because of the enormity of the large and complex data sets the CID seizes, it is necessary need to look for new techniques that make computers perform some analysis tasks, and ideally assist investigators by finding evidence. Recently, CID has developed a new investigation platform called LES[2]. This tool is based on Natural Language Processing (NLP) techniques [1] such as Named Entity Extraction [2] and Information Retrieval (IR) [3] in combining with a visualization model to improve the analysis of a large and complex dataset.

In this paper, we present LES tool (LES) and evaluate the performance of LES because there are very few NLP tools that are being exploited to tackle very large and complex datasets in the context of investigation on white-collar crimes. Indeed, the-oretical understanding of the techniques that are used is necessary. This theoretical review can help explain the usage of these new techniques in criminal investigations, and pinpoint what work needs to be done before the most effective implementation and usage is possible. The rest of this paper is organised as follows: Sect. 2 shows the background of this research including related work in this domain. We present briefly LES and evaluation methods in Sect. 3. We apply our method to analysis the perfor-mance of LES on a distributed platform in Sect. 4. Finally, we conclude and discuss on future work in Sect. 5.

2 Background

2.1 Natural Language Processing in Law Enforcement

NLP implemented techniques can be very useful in a law enforcement environment, especially when unstructured and large amounts of data need to be processed by criminal investigators. Already commonly used techniques like Optical Character Recognition (OCR) [4] and machine translations [5] can be successfully used in criminal investigations. For example OCR is used in fraud investigations to automat-ically transform unstructured invoices and other financial papers into searchable and aggregated spreadsheets. In the past more difficult to implement techniques like automatic summarization of texts, information extraction, entity extraction and rela-tionship extraction [1] are now coming into reach of law enforcement and intelligence agencies. This is manly so because of the decline in cost per processing unit and the fact that these techniques need a large amount of processing power to be able to used effectively.

To zoom in on this a little further: for example the extraction of entities out of large amounts of text can be useful when it is unclear what persons or other entities are

---

[2] Again, real name of the tool cannot be disclosed because of confidential agreement of the project.

involved in a criminal investigation. Combined with a visual representation of the present relations between the extracted entities, this analysis can provide insight in the corresponding (social-) networks between certain entities. Indeed, the usage of NLP techniques to 'predict' criminality, for example grooming by possible paedophiles [6] or trying to determine when hit-and-run crimes may happen by analysing Twitter messages [7] is possible today. A movement from single available NLP techniques like text summarization, text translation, information and relationship extraction towards more intelligent NLP based implementations for law enforcement like crime prediction, crime prevention, criminal intelligence gathering, (social-) network analysis and anomaly detection can be observed in literature. Also theoretical frameworks and models in the field of 'forensic linguistics' [8] are proposed which can be used behind the technical implementation of NLP techniques in criminal investigations.

When (commercial-) solutions using these techniques come available, this could lead to more extensive NLP based law enforcement systems that can handle Crime prediction, deliver automated intelligence on criminal activities, analyse the behaviour of subjects on social networks and detect anomalies in texts or other data. The output of these systems is ideally presented in a visual comprehensible way so the criminal investigator can quickly assess the data and take appropriate action.

2.2 Big Data in Criminal Investigations

No strict definition can be given for the concept Big Data [9] as such, but what can be concluded is that Big Data at least has some common elements and that Big does not necessarily mean large volumes. Complexity and the inner structure of the data are also very important to determine if a dataset belongs to the concept of Big Data or not. Another term that is commonly used when people talk about 'Big Data' is 'Unstructured Data'. As law enforcement we are confronted with at least parts of the Big Data problem; for instance in fraud investigations *the fraud investigation unit* regularly seizes a complete company (network-) environment including cloud storage and all belonging data. Because this data for the *fraud investigation unit* as outsiders is unstructured, and from a variety of sources (computer images, servers, internal communication, wiretap data, databases etc.) these datasets fall under the definition, and elements, of Big Data in terms of volume and complexity (also known as variety of the data). But also a very large e-mail database containing millions of suspect e-mails can fall under the Big Data problem because of the complexity of this data set. Please note that in most descriptions Big Data is measured against three axes: Volume, Variety and Velocity. What we see is that in the *fraud investigation unit's* types of investigation, the focus is mostly on the volume and variety of the large data set. Velocity is not really an issue as they are investigating a static data set. This is so because after seizure the data that needs to be investigated will not (rapidly) change anymore.

What can be said is that the existence of Big Data poses new and unique challenges for law enforcement when evidence needs to be found in an investigation with these characteristics. What also was can be said is that not only the actual size of the total seized data matters, but also the rate of complexity of the data that determines if a case falls under a Big Data definition.

As an example, in a large carousel fraud case that the *fraud investigation unit* investigated in the past, the suspect was a bank that operated from *the fraud investigation unit's* territory and several countries abroad. In this case investigation data was collected and seized from a lot of sources: internet wiretaps, forensic disc images from tens of workstations, user data from server systems, e-mail servers with literally millions of e-mails, company databases, webservers, and the complete banking back-end systems containing all bank transactions. This investigation had the characteristics of Big Data on both levels, a high complexity of the data (the complete banking system had to be reconstructed and analysed) and a high amount of total data (the house searches were in 2006, and in that time a total of 15 Terabyte of data was seized).

This paper is about the usage of NLP techniques in fraud investigations, there are specific characteristics for these types of investigations that determine why another approach towards Big Data investigation is necessary. In fact our *fraud investigation unit* mostly investigates White Collar Crime cases. Most police departments focus on other criminal offenses like murder cases, child abuse, threats, hacking, malware etc. The *fraud investigation unit* on the other hand acts on criminal cases like money laundering, terrorism funding, (tax-) fraud, etc.

This differentiation and specialism results in different "*digital markers*" for White collar crime versus "Police types" of crime where, in general terms, evidence can be found (Fig. 1).

White Collar Crime	Police types of crime
Documents	Files
Networks	Single PC's / Mobile Devices
(Corporate-) Mail	Webmail / Chat
Databases	Cryptography
Company Software	Network analysis
Server environments	File Systems
Backup tapes	Memory analysis
	Unknown services

Fig. 1. Digital Markers for White collar crime and general offenses

For the *fraud investigation unit* this focus on White Collar crime means that the *fraud investigation unit* has to be able to investigate: (i) Complex (unstructured-) datasets; (ii) Large datasets; (iii) Company networks; (iv) Complex communication networks between suspects; (v) Mostly text based evidence.

As you can see, this list shows that the *fraud investigation unit* will encounter Big Data problems *because* of the specific criminal investigation domain, and that the evidence the *fraud investigation unit* gathers is *mostly* text based. Before the introduction of NLP techniques running on the new *fraud investigation unit* platform LES, the *fraud investigation unit* had massive problems with handling the enormous amounts of data that are so specific for white-collar crime investigations. These problems can be summarised in:

- Time taken to process al data that was seized.
- Forensic software not able to handle the huge amounts of data items coming from for instance e-mail databases.
- Crashing software when querying the investigation tooling database, because of overload.
- Unacceptable waiting time for investigators when performing a query on the data (up to 30 min per query).
- Too many search hits to make analysis of the evidence humanly possible in many cases.
- Too much technical approach and interfacing for regular investigators by currently used tooling.

What also can be observed is that most police cases can make use of the Digital Forensics methodology and tooling as is described in literature [10]. Unfortunately the *fraud investigation unit* has to use tooling that is best suitable for criminal investigations falling under Police Types of crime where evidence can be found in/from files, desktop/mobile devices, email, network/memory analysis, etc.

2.3   Related Work

There are very few researches of NLP in the context of Digital Forensics, especially to tackle the problem of Big Data of financial crimes. In the context of Digital Forensics, [11] used NLP techniques to classify of file fragments. In fact, they use support vector machines [12] along with feature vectors consisted of the unigram and bigram counts of bytes in the fragment. The method proposed is efficient; it is however, not in the context of investigating documents related to financial crimes. In [13], authors proposed a corpus of text message data. This corpus can support NLP techniques in investigating data located on mobile devices. This corpus is very useful in analysing short text but it is not for long, complex documents such as MS word document, presentations, spread sheets, etc. Related to the forensics financial crimes, [14] proposed a semantic search based on text mining and information retrieval. Authors however focus on documents from collaboration platform such as e-mail, forum as well as in social networks. Their main objective is how to optimise the searching queries.

3   LES Tool and Method of Evaluation

In this section, we present briefly LES, a NLP based tool that has been developed to study the possibilities and benefits the usage of NLP techniques can provide in complex fraud investigations. Next, we describe the investigating process where we apply LES tool to analyse evidence files. Finally we present methods we used to evaluate this tool.

3.1 LES Tool

Because of the problems of handing Big Data investigations mentioned earlier, our fraud investigation unit decided to develop tooling in-house that would be able to handle these specific types of investigations. The three most important requirements for the new tool are:

- Improving the data processing time, to handle large amounts of data.
- Improving the data analysis time needed, to handle complex datasets.
- Enable end users to perform complex tasks with a very simple interface.

This tool was called LES (Fig. 2) and its main characteristics are:

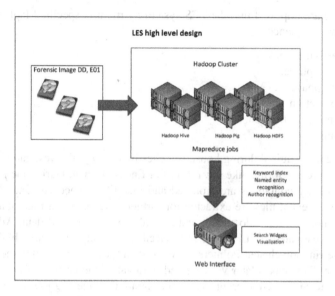

Fig. 2. High level design of LES tool

- Running on an Apache Hadoop platform [15].
- Ability to handle large amounts of data.
- Use NLP techniques to improve evidence finding.
- Visualisation of found (possible-) evidence.
- A simple web based GUI with advanced search capabilities.

In house developed software components allow investigators to rapidly access forensic disk images or copied out single files. MapReduce [16] jobs are then executed over the data to make parallel processing possible over multiple server nodes. Other MapReduce jobs are built in LES tool for text extraction and text indexing. At this moment the following NLP techniques are implemented in LES:

- Information extraction.
- Named Entity Recognition (NER).
- Relationship Extraction.

The Information and NER extraction process uses a combination of techniques to extract useful information: tabular extraction (for lists of known and described entities), regular expression extraction, and the Stanford NER library also known as CRFClassifier [17]. The relationships between entities are arbitrarily determined by the distance between these entities. If a distance is smaller than a threshold, a relationship between two entities is stored in the LES system (a Hadoop cluster of computers running LES tool). This implementation of relationship extraction is based on co-reference between words, which in system tests appears to perform quite well.

3.2 Investigation Process

Evidence files are imported into the LES system by running specific MapReduce jobs in a predefined sequence:

(1) Prepare Evidence.
(2) Extraction phase.
(3) Indexing phase.
(4) NER extraction phase.
(5) Relationship Extraction.
(6) Analysing.

The evidence acquired during house-searches by the digital investigators is mainly recorded in a forensic format like raw *dd* files or Encase format. During the preparation phase the evidence containers are mounted and integrity is checked. Then by default only the most relevant files are extracted for further processing. At this moment these files are the most common document and textual types and e-mail data. All files that need to be investigated by LES tool are placed in a so-called binary 'blob' or data stream on the Hadoop cluster. Pointers to the original files are recorded in the file index on the cluster. This makes later viewing and retrieval of the original file much easier. When all extracted files are present in the data stream the indexing job is run. Next, the NER and RE phase are performed and finally all results are imported in the LES Hadoop Elastic search environment.

3.3 Methodology

Our evaluation method is based on the combination of Microsoft's MSDN performance testing methodology [18], TMap NEXT [19] from Sogeti and some custom evaluation items (quality characteristics). The combination of different methodologies has led to the following concrete test case parameters that were evaluated:

- Test data set processing time, split in time to generate NER, extract relations, generate keyword index.
- Test dataset query response times.
- Accuracy of the data retrieval: cross referencing with standard tooling.
- Data controllability: completeness of the data, evidence integrity and chain of evidence reproducibility.

4 Experiments and Analysis of Results

In this section, we describe firstly a case study we used in our experiments. We also show the platform where we performed our tests. Finally, we present and analyse the results of these experiments.

4.1 Case Study Description

The test dataset is actual case data coming from an investigation against the FB bank that the CID has worked on in the period 2006–2012. This offshore bank was suspected of aiding carousel fraud (also known as MTIC fraud), illegal banking and money laundering. During the height of this fraud an European country lost 400–600 million pounds every month on illegal VAT repayments. All VAT repayments concerned were transferred into FB bank customer accounts. Figure 3 shows the VAT repayments per month in this European country for the period January 2001 until January 2006. In the period our suspect was active the VAT repayments rise significantly (may 2005 until June 2006). After searching in CID, the VAT repayments dropped back to a normal level of 25 million euro per month. At that moment the most important questions that our investigators needed to answer where:

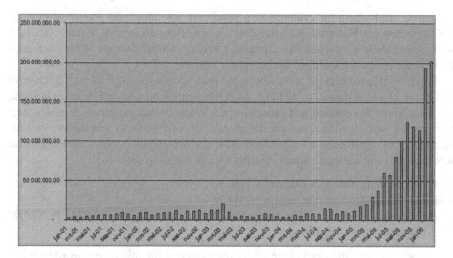

Fig. 3. VAT repayments over FB bank accounts

- Where is the tax money?
- Who is responsible for this carousel fraud?
- How does the money laundering work?
- Is the FB bank an illegal bank in this European country?
- Did the bank management know about this fraud?

To build a case against the suspect's, house searches were performed in September 2006. Not only was the bank's main office in one European country searched, but also locations in other European countries and in North America. During these house searches lots and lots of data was collected. Not only from digital sources, but also a lot of paper was seized. All paper information was processed, scanned and OCR'ed.

4.2   Dataset

The dataset that was used is applicable for the two dimensions Volume and Variety (Complexity) of Big Data. Velocity is not an issue for our experiments at this stage. The data set that is used contains historical data from the period 2006–2012.

The total data set for the FB investigation was 15 Terabyte in size, an extract of the most important data consisted of:

- Total size of dataset: 375 GB.
- Disk images (Encase E01): 292 disk images.
- Microsoft Exchange mail databases: 96 GB.
- Office documents: 481.000.
- E-mails: 1.585.500.
- Total size of documents to investigate: 156 GB.
- Total size of extracted textual data: 21 GB.

As we are looking for evidence in a fraud case we can expect that most incriminating content can be found in textual data, coming from documents, e-mails etc. LES will automatically extract all files containing textual information out of file containers like Encase images, Exchange databases, zip files etc.

Next, from these files all text is extracted leading to a total size of pure flat text of 21 GB out of a total dataset of 375 GB. As this investigation was performed in the past, we today know that finding and processing the evidence that was needed, took a total of six years investigation. Because the amount of total items to investigate, and the complexity of this dataset, the time needed for this investigation took a lot longer than was thought of at the start. Some statistics can be found as follows:

- Evidence items found in dataset: 2.718.
- Total textual items in test dataset: 2.144.254.
- Percentage of evidence found versus total textual items: 0,126 % (2718/ 2.144.254) × 100 = 0,126 %).

As we can see, the percentage of usable evidence for this case was only 0,126 percent. This indicates the needle in the haystack problem we are facing for these types of investigations.

4.3   Testing Platform

The testing system is a cluster consists of 14 physical servers with the following roles:

- 2x Hadoop Namenode (for redundancy purposes).

- 6x Hadoop Datanode (to store the data on).
- 1x Hadoop Edgenode (for cluster management).
- 4x Index nodes (to process the data).
- 1x webserver (for the end-user GUI).

Hadoop processing and storage:

- 18 TB storage.
- 24 cores Intel Xeon E5504.

Index nodes processing and storage:

- 12 TB storage.
- 12 cores Intel Xeon E5504.

Total cluster internal memory is 256 GB. The cluster has been build and configured according to the Hadoop recommendations for building a Hadoop cluster.

4.4 Evaluation Criteria

We applied different criteria to LES tool. These criteria are divided in four groups: performance acceptance, functionality, user-friendly interface and specific requirements.

Performance acceptance criteria relate to the processing time, query response time, evidence items and NER relation diagram:

- The processing time includes time taken to generate NLP NER database, time taken to generate keyword index, time taken to generate edges and nodes database for visualization, system time taken to find evidence items (using adaptive query interface) and time taken to find evidence items (using NER and NER diagram).
- Two metrics are taken into account in query response time: keyword based search response time and combination of keywords response time.
- For evidence items, we look at the total amount of items to investigate, amount of items dropped or lost and amount of items per file type.
- For the NER relation diagram, we focus on time taken to generate diagram and time taken to adjust levels.

In terms of the functionality acceptance, we look at two main characters: data controllability and flexibility.

- Data controllability including (i) completeness of the processed data check; (ii) chain of evidence correctness; (iii) evidence integrity and (iv) reproducibility of found evidence.
- Flexibility including (i) number of search paths towards evidence item; (ii) number of search methods supported and (iii) number of ways to present data.

In order to evaluate the user friendliness, we run the survey on the end users. Finally, we evaluate NER relevance for case and NER diagram relevance for case as specific requirements in the performance evaluation of our approach.

4.5 Result Description and Analysis

We evaluate all the performance perspective of LES tool with different criteria described in Sect. 4.4. In general terms we expect the following result of LES running on the testing data:

- Less time needed for extracting textual information from files and forensic images.
- Less time needed to make a keyword based index.
- A NLP named entity extraction from the data set.
- A NLP relationship file generated from the data set.
- A graphical representation of NLP relations.
- Faster query response time than using traditional tools.
- More paths towards evidence items.
- Faster pinpointing of evidence in a large dataset.

We also compare the processing time between Forensic Toolkit (FTK) [20] and LES tool on the same testing dataset. FTK has been configured in such a way that it approached the LES way of processing data the most. That means that all images and container items were read in FTK, but all extra options were disabled to make comparison fairer (Fig. 2). As you can see, FTK has been configured to not perform Entropy test, carving, OCR. Indeed, only possible textual files were added as evidence to the case (documents, spreadsheets, e-mail messages). Only from this selection FTK was allowed to make a keyword based index (Fig. 4).

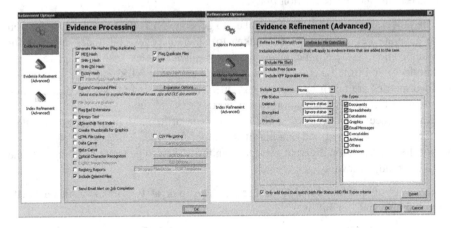

Fig. 4. FTK case configuration

4.5.1 Processing Time

First of all, we discuss on the processing time of LES. As mentioned above, the processing time is broken down in three main parts.

- Time taken to process test data $T1$. In fact, this is time taken for text extraction and it takes LES tool 34 min to complete i.e. $T1 = 34$ min.

- Time taken to generate NLP NER databases *T2*. We evaluate of the total time taken to generate the Named Entity database based on the test data set. The named entity database is an essential part of the LES NLP implementation, and is used to enhance the evidence retrieval possibilities for investigators. The time taken to generate the NLP NER database is measured on the LES cluster for the testing data set. System monitoring is performed by the Ganglia system monitoring service. So in our experiment, *T2* is 38 min with 11.008.100 entities (edges) were extracted. Note that this test also includes the generation of edges and nodes databases.
- Time taken to generate keyword index *T3*. In this test, we look at the total time taken to generate the searchable keyword index based on the test data set in LES tool and the *T3* is 12 min.

Briefly, the total processing time of LES tool T is a sum of T1, T2 and T3 and it is 1 h and 34 min (T = T1 + T2 + T3 = 34 min + 38 min + 12 min). According to the FTK processing log, the FTK processing time of the testing dataset, with the criteria shown above is 10 h and 54 min.

Next, we look at time taken to find evidence items by using adaptive z interface. For this evaluation we are using our known evidence items as reference items to find in LES. We also use the chosen keywords as shown in response time test (Sect. 4.5.2, Table 3) and add up the time needed for the system to present the correct evidence item from the test data set. The total time response and retrieval test is used for the FTK results to compare with our performance. Table 1 describes the comparison the performance of LES tool and FTK.

Table 1. Time taken to find evidence items using adaptive query interface (in seconds)

Document	FTK	LES
D-195 (.msg)	35.1	0.5
D-550 (.ppt)	29.2	0.5
D-718 (.xls)	28	0.5
D-735 (.msg)	16	0.5
D-805 (.txt)	20	0.5

We evaluate time taken to find evidence items not only by using adaptive query interface but also by using NER and NER diagram. Basically, in LES tool, the extracted named entities can be selected to find the needed evidence. A combination of these entities should find the evidence items in a certain amount of time. To evaluate it, we select entities from the known evidence items, and query LES on the same extracted entities. Making a combination of entities that will show the relevant evidence items. From our known evidence items the NLP extracted entities [NAME1], [NAME2], [NAME3], [NAME4] and [NAME5] were used as input for the NER query to search on. Table 2 shows the result of this test.

The system extracted the known named entities automatically and created the links to the known evidence files. What is interesting is that the determination if an entity is a person, location or organization is not always correct. The retrieval of the evidence items is all handled under 0, 5 s by LES. In fact, the LES tool was evaluated by running

Table 2. Time taken to find evidence items using NER and NER diagram

Entity	Hits	Response time (second)	NER identified as
[NAME1]	24279	0.330	PERSON
[NAME2]	1006	0.420	PERSON, LOCATION, ORGANISATION
[NAME3]	1867	0.142	PERSON
[NAME4]	1	0.045	PERSON
[NAME5]	3439	0.358	PERSON

various experiments on the testing datasets. As we can see, the overall processing time of this tool is 6 times faster than FTK with the same testing datasets. Furthermore, when LES is configured to only create a keyword-based index, similar to Forensic Toolkit, the LES tool is even 11 times faster than FTK running on the same datasets. LES does however need extra processing time to perform the needed NLP calculations, but enhances the ease of finding evidence by running these NLP processes.

4.5.2   Query Response Time

Regarding to the performance acceptance criteria, we evaluate moreover the query response time including the keyword base search response time and the combination of key words response time. Response times of LES tool are significantly better when it is used to search through the test data by single keywords. Table 3 shows the response time of keyword searching. FTK shows some remarkable slow response times when

Table 3. Response time of single keyword search

Document	Keywords	FTK		LES	
		Response time (s)	Retrieve time (s)	Response time (s)	Retrieve time (s)
D-195	Discontinue	6	27	0.005	<0.5
(.msg)	Fraud	3	41	0.078	<0.5
	Revenue	6	287	0.119	<0.5
D-550	Scrubbing	6	17	0.081	<0.5
(.ppt)	Blacklists	5	14	0.099	<0.5
	Violation	6	365	0.069	<0.5
D-718	[NAME1]	18	295	0.138	<0.5
(.xls)	Training	6	383	0.143	<0.5
	Crime control	7	4	0.195	<0.5
D-735	[NAME2]	3	22	0.006	<0.5
(.msg)	[NAME3]	5	52	0.023	<0.5
	New York	5	195	0.141	<0.5
D-805	[NAME4]	5	4	0.038	<0.5
(.txt)	Bermuda	5	1190	0.091	<0.5
	[NAME5]	5	33	0.020	<0.5

using single keywords to search for, whereas LES in most cases is a factor 1000 or faster when searching through the data.

Furthermore, the retrieval times in LES tool are always under 0.5 s, but cannot be shown in a counter, and therefore difficult to give an exact count in milliseconds.

However, this is not a very efficient approach to find unique evidence items, most of the time using only one keyword leads to long lists of results. Also, it is very difficult to make up the best fitting keyword to find the evidence. Normally a combination of keywords or multiple search iterations is used, but in practice our investigators start hypothesis building by trying single keywords and see what comes back as a result. What can be seen from the FTK evaluation is that when using single keywords when trying to pinpoint evidence, the retrieval time can be very long. When using single keywords only and keywords are not chosen well or are not unique enough, waiting time becomes unacceptable long from an end-user perspective when we choose a response time of 20 s maximum. Of course investigators also need to be trained to perform smart search actions when using FTK. It is essential to choose keyword combinations well. Next, we use the five known evidence items to locate and use an AND combination of keywords to evaluate response time and retrieval time of evidence items. Table 4 shows the results of this experiment.

Table 4. Response time of combined keyword search

Document	Keywords	FTK		LES	
		Response time (s)	Retrieve time (s)	Response time (s)	Retrieve time (s)
D-195 (.msg)	Discontinue, fraud, revenue	28	7.1	0.006	<0.5
D-550 (.ppt)	Scrubbing, blacklists, violation	24	5.2	0.138	<0.5
D-718 (.xls)	[NAME1], training crime control	10	18	0.195	<0.5
D-735 (.msg)	[NAME2], [NAME3], NewYork	11	5	0.232	<0.5
D-805 (.txt)	[NAME4], Bermuda, [NAME5]	16	4	0.004	<0.5

When a combination of keywords is used we see that the response times for FTK are worse than single keyword search. On the other hand, using multiple keywords in LES the response time is also milliseconds for the performed evaluations. From an end-user perspective a response in milliseconds is more or less instant and thus leading to a better investigation experience. When the various NLP techniques are used to search for evidence, the LES tool response times are also in milliseconds. For instance the selection of named entities and the drawing of a relation diagram are performed very fast by the system.

4.5.3   Evidence Items

Next, we evaluate the total amount of processed evidence items per file type analysing system and processing log files for FTK and LES (Table 5).

Table 5. Total number of processed evidence items per file type

Document type	Number of items per file type	
	FTK	LES
Email	1.585.500	1.641.063
Word documents	44.105	44.837
Spreadsheets	68.101	38.580
Presentations	6.548	2620

As we are not sure how FTK counts evidence items, and which types are counted and which are not, it is difficult to draw a conclusion from these figures. But what we do know is that FTK counts for instance every OLE object item as a unique evidence item for Microsoft Office documents. So that increases the count for FTK significantly. However, since we have found all our randomly selected evidence items in both FTK and LES we can be carefully positive that no essential data is lost in LES.

4.5.4   Data Controllability

Looking at the functionality perspective, LES has more possible search paths towards an evidence item; this could mean that evidence can be found faster using LES, because an investigator has more chance 'hitting' a useful search path. This coincides with the fact that in LES evidence can be found in more ways, because more search methods are implemented. These search methods increase the ways investigators can search for evidence. Especially the implemented NLP entity selection in combination with other search methods creates new evidence finding possibilities that previously were not possible. When looking at the data presentation parts of the software evaluation we can see that LES has more ways of presenting data to the investigator; the visualization view of found evidence can help investigators finding new leads.

We investigate moreover how the chain of evidence is maintained and what guarantees are built in the software to maintain the chain of evidence. Eventually, we evaluate the evidence handling in FTK and LES. What information has to be recorded for evidence items, how strong is the logging mechanism behind the tooling, etc. For FTK, it operates according to known forensic procedures and standards. FTK supports: Media sanitation, Write protection, Verification of evidence, Forensic copy abilities and forensic analyses. For all these parts extensive logging is provided. In short we can conclude that FTK is able to supports maintaining the needed chain of evidence for handling criminal investigations. Regarding to LES, as it has been built from another perspective, the extensiveness of maintaining the chain of evidence is less than FTK. LES does however try to maintain at least essential parts to keep the chain of evidence in tact:

- Supporting forensic image formats
- Logging of data processing
- Logging of user activity, including search queries performed by the user
- Hashing of files that are included in the case
- Maintaining original path to file locations, and displaying file offsets

Another important functional part is the integrity of evidence. In fact we check hash values for the known evidence files. File hashes for the known evidence items are calculated with an external hash value calculator and compared with the hash value reported in LES and FTK. Throughout this test, both LES and FTK have all hash values matches.

Related to the data controllability, we also evaluate the reproducibility of found evidence. This evaluation is to find out if an evidence item can be traced back to the original source easily. This is essential to keep the chain of evidence intact. The selected evidence items are used to check if they can be traced back to the original source and how the tool supports this. For FTK, it supports logging, hashing and keeping record of original file offset, path and belonging container (image). With FTK it is easy to trace back to the original place of a file or evidence item. Also reports can be generated where the original location is included. For a thorough forensic investigation process, this is a must have. Using these reports it is also easy to use another tool to check the results of FTK. In our experiments, all five selected evidence items were found and could be traced back to the original source using the FTK interface. Regarding to LES, it only records the original file path and file offset if possible together with the analysed evidence file. In LES the original path can be seen for the known evidence files, also the file offset is reported if the file is coming from an image file. To retrace the file in the original container, external software is necessary, like FTK or Encase.

Briefly, what can be seen is that FTK has better data control embedded, thus in FTK the chain of evidence is maintained more thoroughly. Also, FTK has better file control embedded; tracing back a file to its originating location is better implemented in FTK than in LES, thus the chain of evidence is maintained better.

4.5.5   Flexibility

As mentioned in Sect. 4.4, we focus on the number of search paths toward evidence item, the number of search methods supported and the number of ways to present data in order to evaluate the flexibility of LES. The number of search paths is the amount of possible search paths towards an evidence item determines how 'easy' it is to find a specific item. The more paths you have towards an evidence item the higher the chance that you will find the evidence needed. In this experiment, we take into account the specific search paths that are available in FTK and LES. The possible search paths in FTK include (i) browsing through tree; (ii) keyword search (combination) and (iii) filtering on the file characteristics (type, date/time, etc.). If all three items could be used alone or in combination with each other a total of 6 combinations are possible. On the other hand, the possible search paths in LES include (i) keyword search combination; (ii) filtering on file characteristics (type, date/time etc.); (iii) using NLP NER list and (iv) using NLP NER diagram. If all four items could be used alone or in combination with each other a total of 24 combinations are possible. As LES will add additional search paths because of the implementation of new NLP techniques in the near future this probably will lead to an increase in total search paths for LES. By adding new search methods, the total amount of search paths also increases. Possibly this could lead to investigators finding needed evidence quicker and more efficient.

Looking at the number of search methods supported, FTK only supports the keyword-based search. LES tool moreover can support both keyword-based search and NLP, NER based search.

Finally, FTK can display data on the 6 ways: List view, Tree view, Document preview, Categories view, Evidence item view and Search view. LES can display data on the 7 ways: List view, Document preview, Categories view, Evidence item view, NER view, NER relations diagram view and Search view. This evaluation item generally describes the way information is presented towards the investigator. Of course FTK has various sub-views that can be used, but only the most used views are counted, and the most technical views are neglected, as these are not relevant for CID investigators in general. Also, FTK has a much more technical presentation of data, where LES data views are more focused on non-technical investigators.

4.5.6   User-Friendly

LES is specifically designed to help the end-user (in this case the CID investigators) search through Big Data more easily. As the CID process differs from technical forensic investigations, LES has to deliver a different end-user experience. The CID investigators have no technical IT background, but do need to be able to analyze complex and large Big Data in the most fitting and comfortable way. To evaluate LES, we look at (i) Analyse the end-user preferred way of looking at data; (ii) Investigate what functionality is needed to suit the FIOD investigators needs in Big Data investigation and (iii) Analyse the end-user preferred GUI setup.

We have performed this evaluation with the help of an external contractor who set-up various usability sessions. Investigators from the CID were asked to show how they analyse data at this moment, and how they would like to work in the future. In another session a real-time GUI mock-up was constructed with live input from the CID investigators. During this session people could ask the GUI mock-up builder to add or remove elements from the mock-up, or to change the position of GUI items on the screen. Then an initial GUI was built with mock-up functionality that was evaluated by letting CID investigators use this GUI mock-up. The investigators were filmed during- and interviewed after this session. This resulted in a final GUI and LES functionality report. All attendant investigators agree that this tool resulted in a very good combination of technology push of NLP techniques and LES backend together with an end-user view of how fraud investigations need to be performed.

4.5.7   Specific Requirements

We evaluate moreover if the extracted named entities have significance for the known data set. To do so, we select the top 100 most extracted entities over the whole data set. Determine if these entities are relevant for the known case. Someone with enough knowledge of the case can only perform this. Also, use the five known evidence items to see if the extracted named entities belonging to these items relate to other known entities coming from other documents. When selecting the top 100 entities of type PERSON a list is generated with these entities. This list was analyzed against the background of the known case, and the conclusion is that the list covers the most important persons that were involved in this case. This indicates that an aggregation of extracted entities is relevant for the known data set. In fact, it is interesting to see that without prior knowledge a list of persons can be automatically generated out of a data set. In this case the produced list was also relevant for the criminal investigation. In new cases this could mean that running such a query can help identifying unknown players in the investigation.

4.5.8   Further Discussion

A big advantage of LES is that LES has been developed with the end-user in mind, in this case a financial and fraud investigator who needs to investigate a Big Data set. Specifically the LES query interface is very flexible and helps analyzing complex and large data sets, especially the possibility to add query windows (widgets) and refine searches by doing that is very powerful.

Specific evaluation requirements that were mostly focused on the implementation and usage of NLP techniques show that the implemented NLP techniques can help investigators finding evidence in another way, possibly faster and more efficient. At the minimum a new view towards complex data is presented for investigators. LES requires less search iterations to find evidence, because of the implementation of NLP NER and visualisation of evidence. On the other hand, FTK's keyword based search requires investigators to work through more data and refine search queries a lot of times. For example, Fig. 5 shows the search results of keyword "Obama". What you can see here is that LEWIS highlights the search term "Obama" yellow. The purple circles are still the documents that contain the named entity "Obama". And all blue dots are other entities in relation with "Obama", like "Clinton", "Qaida" etc. Indeed, when interested in a document, the user only has to double click on the purple circle to show the document, or click on a related entity to adjust the search parameters.

Besides, some noteworthy points that also came up during the evaluation were for instance that it was difficult to find literature that evaluates AccessData forensic toolkit on a performance and data controllability level. It looks like this tooling has not been evaluated very thoroughly yet by a respectable authority. For Hadoop/MapReduce techniques we found that the usage of a Hadoop cluster seems to be very efficient when one needs to process large amounts of textual data. However, the programming paradigm of Hadoop/MapReduce are more complex than regular programming problems because of the distributed and multi-processing nature of the Hadoop cluster. The issues that we found during the evaluation were that a (too-) large edges and nodes file leads to graphical representation problems. Too much named entities and extracted relations leads to information overload for the end-user. The forensic chain of evidence is more difficult to maintain in LES. This is because of the nature of LES' inner workings, and the fact that it extracts textual information out of forensic images.

At organization level, we found that the CID will need to explain the difference between forensic computer investigation and analysis of Big Data. When to use what tool all depends on the type of investigation, the needed evidence, and the amount and complexity of the data. As the CID mainly has large fraud cases, a logical choice would

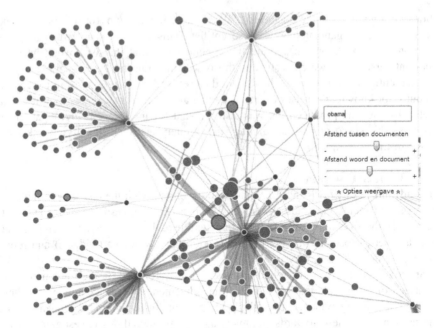

Fig. 5. LES visualisation search "obama"

be to use LES as the preferred tool for these kinds of investigations. One remark that must be made is that all data found in LES must be verified using a (forensic-) tool until LES has a proven track record in court of law.

As a conclusion, the usage of LES tool that uses NLP as key enabler to handle very large and complex data investigations. This means LES tool improves the 'white collar crime' investigation process in terms of speed and efficiency.

5   Conclusions and Future Work

In this paper, we present and evaluate LES tool that is based on NLP techniques to help criminal investigators handle large amounts of textual information. In fact, we evaluate different perspectives of LES tools. In terms of speed: the proposed solution is significantly faster in handling complex (textual) data sets in less time compared to traditional forensics approach. In terms of efficiency: the proposed solution is optimized for the fraud investigation process. The usage of NLP techniques helps in optimizing the investigation process. Investigators have more possibilities finding evidence in very large and complex dataset, aided by smart NLP based techniques. This greatly improves fraud investigation efficiency.

Some topics for further scientific and practical research is coming up. In terms of LES tool, more functions have being added such as automatic summarisation of texts, author recognition, detection of cover language, detection of communication patterns, language detection, adding fraud domain knowledge to a NLP language corpus [21], visualisation of searching results, etc. In order to handle efficiently the fraud domain knowledge we also consider using the knowledge map [22, 23]. We are moreover working on the integration this tool with our anti-money laundering solution [24, 25].

References

1. Liddy Elizabeth, D.: Natural language processing, 2nd edn. In: Encyclopedia of Library and Information Science. Marcel Decker, Inc., New York (2001)
2. Tjong, K.S., Erik, F.: Introduction to the CoNLL-2003 shared task: language-independent named entity recognition. In: Proceedings of the Conference on Natural Language Learning, June 2003, Edmonton, Canada (2003)
3. Rijsbergen, C.J.: Information Retrieval, 2nd edn. Butteworths, London (1979)
4. Lais, S.: Quick Study: Optical Character Recognition. Computer World. http://www.computerworld.com/s/article/73023/Optical_Character_Recognition. Accessed 25 Jun 2014
5. http://www.systransoft.com/systran/corporate-profile/translation-technology/what-is-machine-translation/. Accessed 25 Jun 2014
6. Jurafsky, D., Martin James, H.: Speech and Language Processing - An Introduction to Natural Language Processing, 2nd edn. Stanford University, University of Colorado at Boulder, Pearson Prentice Hall (2009)
7. Fromkin, V., Rodman, R., Hyam, N.: An Introduction to language, 9th edn. Wadsworth, Boston (2011)
8. Rafferty, A.N., de Marneffe, M.-C., Manning, C.D.: Finding Contradictions in Text. ACL 2008. http://nlp.stanford.edu/pubs/contradiction-acl08.pdf. Accessed 25 Jun 2014
9. Sokol, L., Ames, R.: Analytics in a Big Data Environment. IBM Redbooks (2012)
10. Innis Tasha, R., et al.: Towards applying text mining and natural language processing for biomedical ontology acquisition. In: TMBIO 2006: Proceedings of the 1st international Workshop on Text Mining in Bioinformatics, pp. 7–14 (2006)
11. Fitzgerald, S., et al.: Using NLP techniques for file fragment classification. Digital Invest. **9**, 44–49 (2012)
12. Scholkopf, B.: A short tutorial on kernels. Technical report MSR-TR-200-6t, Microsoft Research (2000)
13. O'Day, D.R., Calix, R.A.: Text message corpus: applying natural language processing to mobile device forensics. In: IEEE International Conference on Multimedia and Expo, 5–9 July 2013, San Jose, USA (2013)
14. Van Dijk, D., Henseler, H.: Semantic search in e-Discovery: an interdisciplinary approach. In: Workshop on Standards for Using Predictive Coding, Machine Learning, and Other Advanced Search and Review Methods in E-Discovery, ICAIL 2013
15. http://hadoop.apache.org. Accessed 25 Jun 2014
16. Dean, J., Ghemawat, S.: MapReduce: simplified data processing on large clusters. In: OSDI 2004: Sixth Symposium on Operating System Design and Implementation, December 2004, San Francisco, CA (2004)
17. Popowitch, F.: Using text mining and natural language processing for health care claims processing. ACM SIGKDD Explor. Newsl. - Natural language processing and text mining **7** (1), 59–66 (2005)
18. Meier, J.D., et al.: Microsoft Performance Testing Guidance for Web Applications. Redmond (2007). http://msdn.microsoft.com/en-us/library/bb924375.aspx
19. Buist, A.H., Kraaij, W., Raaijmakers, S.: Automatic summarization of meeting data: a feasibility study. In: Proceedings of the 15th CLIN Conference (2005)

20. http://www.accessdata.com/solutions/digital-forensics/ftk. Accessed 25 Jun 2014
21. Norvig, P.: Natural language corpus data. In: Beautiful Data, pp. 219–242 (2009)
22. Le-Khac, N.-A., Aouad, L.M., Kechadi M.-T., Knowledge map: toward a new approach supporting the knowledge management in distributed data mining, KUI track. In: 3rd IEEE International Conference on Autonomic and Autonomous Systems, 19–25 June 2007. Computer Society Press, Athens (2007)
23. Le-Khac, N.-A., Aouad, L.M., Kechadi M.-T.: Distributed knowledge map for mining data on grid platform. Int. J. Comput. Sci. Netw. Secur. 7(10), 98 (2007). ISSN 1738-7906
24. Le-Khac, N.-A., Kechadi, M.-T.: Apply data mining and natural computing in detecting suspicious cases of money laundering in an investment bank: a case study. In: The 10th IEEE International Conference on Data Mining, 14–17 December 2010, Sydney, Australia (2010)
25. Le-Khac, N.-A., et al.: An efficient search tool for an anti-money laundering application of an multi-national bank's dataset. In: International Conference on Information and Knowledge Engineering, 13–16 July 2009, Las Vegas, USA (2009)

Data Leakage Analysis of the Hibernate Query Language on a Propositional Formulae Domain

Raju Halder[1]([✉]), Angshuman Jana[1], and Agostino Cortesi[2]

[1] Indian Institute of Technology Patna, Patna, India
{halder,ajana.pcs13}@iitp.ac.in
[2] Università Ca' Foscari Venezia, Venice, Italy
cortesi@unive.it

Abstract. This paper presents an information flow analysis of Hibernate Query Language (HQL). We define a concrete semantics of HQL and we lift the semantics on an abstract domain of propositional formulae. This way, we capture variables dependences at each program point. This allows us to identify illegitimate information flow by checking the satisfiability of propositional formulae with respect to a truth value assignment based on their security levels.

Keywords: Hibernate query language · Information flow analysis · Abstract interpretation

1 Introduction

Modern database applications are mostly implemented using Object Oriented Programming (OOP) languages supported by relational databases at the back end. Due to paradigm mismatch, the way to access data in object oriented languages is fundamentally different than that in case of relational database languages. Hibernate, an Object Relational Mapping (ORM) framework, mitigates this impedance mismatch problem by replacing direct persistence-related database accesses with high-level object handling functions. Hibernate provides Hibernate Query Language (HQL) which allows SQL-like queries to be written against Hibernate's data objects. Various methods in "Session" interface are used to propagate object's states from memory to the database (or vice versa). Hibernate will detect any change made to an object in persistent state and synchronizes the state with the database when the unit of work completes. A HQL query is translated by Hibernate into a set of conventional SQL queries during run time which in turn performs actions on the database. This way, HQL provides a unified platform for the programmers to develop object-oriented applications to interact with databases, without knowing much details about the underlying databases [5,6,15].

Secure information flow is comprised of two related aspects: information confidentiality and information integrity. Confidentiality refers to limiting the access and disclosure of sensitive information to authorized users only. For instance,

© Springer-Verlag Berlin Heidelberg 2016
A. Hameurlain et al. (Eds.): TLDKS XXIII, LNCS 9480, pp. 23–44, 2016.
DOI: 10.1007/978-3-662-49175-1_2

when we purchase something online, our private data, e.g. credit card number, must be sent only to the merchant without disclosing to any third person during the transmission. Dually, the notion of integrity indicates that data or messages cannot be modified undetectably by any unauthorized person [34].

While access control and encryption prevent confidential information from being read or modified by unauthorized users at source level, they do not regulate the information propagation after it has been released for execution. Confidentiality may be compromised during the flow of information along the control structure of any software systems [29]. Assuming variables 'h' and 'l' are private and public respectively, the following code fragments depict two different scenarios (explicit/direct flow and implicit/indirect flow) of information leakage:

```
l := h                    Explicit/Direct flow
if(h=0) l:=5; else l:=10;   Implicit/Indirect flow
```

Observe that confidential value in 'h' can be deduced by attackers observing 'l' on the output channel.

A wide range of language-based techniques are proposed in the past decades to analyze this illegitimate flow in software products [4,9,16,21,24,28,29,32]. Works in this direction have been starting with the pioneering work of Dennings in the 1970s [13]. As a starting point, the analysis classifies the program variables into various security classes. The simplest one is to consider two: Public/Low (denoted L) and Private/High (denoted H). Considering a mathematical lattice-model of security classes with order $L \leq H$, the secure information flow policy is defined on the lattice: an upward-flow in the lattice is only permissible to preserve confidentiality. Dually, in case of integrity, the lattice-model labels the variables as Tainted (denoted T) and Untainted (denoted U), and follows a dual flow-policy.

The correctness is guaranteed by respecting the non-interference principle that says "a variation of confidential data does not cause any variation to public data": *Given a program P and set of states Σ. The non-interference policy states that $\forall \sigma_1, \sigma_2 \in \Sigma. \sigma_1 \equiv_L \sigma_2 \implies [\![P]\!]\sigma_1 \equiv_L [\![P]\!]\sigma_2$, where $[\![.]\!]$ is semantic function and $\equiv_L$ represents low-equivalence relation between states.*

Most of the notable works which refer to imperative, object-oriented, functional, database query languages, etc. [8,18,21,24,27–29] can not be applied directly to the case of HQL due to the presence and interaction of high-level HQL variables and database attributes through Session methods. Moreover, as we are interested on persistent data, analyzing object-oriented features of HQL does not meet our objectives neither. Let us illustrate a motivating example depicted in Fig. 1. Two POJO classes c_1 and c_2 correspond to two underlying database-tables by mapping class-fields into table-attributes. In the main method of Service Class ExClass, values of the table corresponding to c_1 are used to make a list, and for each element of the list an update is performed on the table corresponding to the class c_2. Observe that there is an information-flow from confidential (denoted by h) to public variables (denoted by l). In fact, the confidential database information h_1 which is extracted at statement 15, affects the public view of the database information l_2 at statement 20. This fact is depicted in Fig. 1(d). The new challenge in this scenario *w.r.t.* state-of-the-art of information leakage detection is that we need to consider both application variables and SQL variables (corresponding to the database attributes).

In this paper[1], we extend the abstract interpretation-based framework in [34] to the case of HQL, focussing on `Session` methods which act as persistent manager. This allows us to perform leakage analysis of sensitive database information when is accessed through high-level HQL code.

The main contributions in this paper are:

- Defining the concrete and an abstract transition semantics of HQL, by using symbolic domain of positive propositional formulae.
- Analyzing possible information leakage based on the abstract semantics, focussing on variable dependences of database attributes on high-level HQL variables.

The structure of the paper is as follows: Sect. 2 briefly discusses the related works in the literature. In Sect. 3, we define the abstract syntax of HQL in BNF. In Sects. 4 and 5, we formalize the concrete and an abstract transition semantics of HQL, by using the symbolic domain of positive propositional formulae. In Sect. 6, we perform information leakage analysis of programs based on the abstract semantics which captures possible leakage of confidential data. Section 7 concludes the paper.

2   Related Works

A comprehensive survey on language-based information-flow analysis is reported in [29]. Most popular static analysis techniques are based on type systems [29, 32, 33], dependence graphs [7, 19–21, 23, 24, 26], formal approaches [1, 2, 14, 22, 34, 35], etc. Besides the conservative nature of static analysis, the run-time monitoring systems detect unauthorized information flow dynamically; however, precision of the analysis completely depends on the execution overload, and of course, it is very prone to false negative [3, 31].

The security type system considers various security types (*e.g.*, *low* and *high*) and a collection of typing rules which determine the type of expressions/commands to guarantee a secure information flow [29, 32, 33]. Some of the typing rules from [29] are mentioned below:

- Expression Type: $\dfrac{}{\vdash exp\colon high}$ $\dfrac{h \notin \mathtt{Var}(exp)}{\vdash exp\colon low}$
- Explicit-flow Rules: $\dfrac{}{[pc] \vdash h := exp}$ $\dfrac{\vdash exp\colon low}{[low] \vdash l := exp}$
- Implicit-flow Rules: $\dfrac{\vdash exp\colon pc \quad [pc] \vdash c_1 \quad [pc] \vdash c_2}{[pc] \vdash if\ exp\ then\ c_1\ else\ c_2}$ $\dfrac{\vdash exp\colon pc \quad [pc] \vdash c}{[pc] \vdash while\ exp\ do\ c}$
- Subsumption Rule: $\dfrac{[high] \vdash c}{[low] \vdash c}$

---

[1] This work is a revised and extended version of [10].

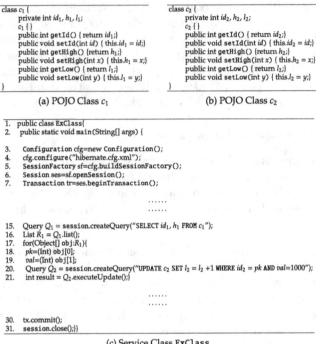

```
class c₁ {                                          class c₂ {
    private int id₁, h₁, l₁;                            private int id₂, h₂, l₂;
    c₁ { }                                              c₂ { }
    public int getId() { return id₁;}                  public int getId() { return id₂;}
    public void setId(int id) { this.id₁ = id;}        public void setId(int id) { this.id₂ = id;}
    public int getHigh() {return h₁;}                  public int getHigh() {return h₂;}
    public void setHigh(int x) { this.h₁ = x;}         public void setHigh(int x) { this.h₂ = x;}
    public int getLow() { return l₁;}                  public int getLow() { return l₂;}
    public void setLow(int y) { this.l₁ = y;}          public void setLow(int y) { this.l₂ = y;}
}                                                   }
```

(a) POJO Class c_1 (b) POJO Class c_2

```
1.   public class ExClass{
2.   public static void main(String[] args) {

3.      Configuration cfg=new Configuration();
4.      cfg.configure("hibernate.cfg.xml");
5.      SessionFactory sf=cfg.buildSessionFactory();
6.      Session ses=sf.openSession();
7.      Transaction tr=ses.beginTransaction();

            ......
            ......

15.     Query Q₁ = session.createQuery("SELECT id₁, h₁ FROM c₁");
16.     List R₁ = Q₁.list();
17.     for(Object[] obj:R₁){
18.        pk=(Int) obj[0];
19.        val=(Int) obj[1];
20.        Query Q₂ = session.createQuery("UPDATE c₂ SET l₂ = l₂ +1 WHERE id₂ = pk AND val=1000");
21.        int result = Q₂.executeUpdate();}

            ......
            ......

30.     tx.commit();
31.     session.close();}}
```

(c) Service Class ExClass

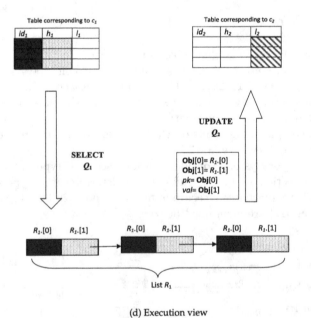

(d) Execution view

Fig. 1. A motivating HQL program P and its execution view

The notation $[pc]$ denotes the security context which can be either $[low]$ or $[high]$. According to the subsumption rule, if a program is typable in a high context then it is also typable in a low context. This allows to reset the program security context to low after a high conditional or a loop.

Although type-based approach is provably sound, but a major drawback is the lack of expressiveness. Moreover, it is not flow-sensitive which may produce false alarm. For instance, consider the following code:

```
①  if(h=1) then
②        l:= 10;
③  else l:= 5;
      ......
⑦  l:= 0;
⑧  output l;
```

Although the program is secure with respect to the classical noninterference principle as the output is always zero, but the type-based approach produces false alarm according to the implicit-flow rule.

As information flow is closely related to the dependence information of programs, the notion of Program Dependence Graph (PDG) is used widely to capture illegitimate flow in programs [7,19–21,24]. As PDGs are flow-sensitive, the analysis improves $w.r.t.$ the type-based approach. For instance, in PDG-based approaches, the above code is secure as there is no path $① \overset{*}{\rightarrow} ⑧$ in the corresponding PDG. Various extensions of PDG exist, for example System Dependence Graph (SDG) in case of inter-procedural call to capture context-sensitivity, Class Dependence Graph (ClDG) in case of Object-Oriented Languages to capture object-sensitivity on dynamic dispatch, etc [20]. Once the dependence graph of a program is constructed, static analysis is performed on the graph to identify the presence of possible insecure flow. An worth mentioning approach is backward slicing which collects all possible paths (or source-nodes) influencing (directly/indirectly) the observable nodes: to be secure, the levels of variables in a path must not exceed the levels of observable variables in the output-node of that path. In other words, slicing helps to partition any insecure program (as a whole) in to secure and insecure part [7]. Semantics-based improvement (*e.g.* path-conditions) is also proposed to disregard semantically unreachable paths [20].

Approaches based on formal techniques, *e.g.* Abstract Interpretation theory, Hoare Logic, Model Checking, etc. are proposed in [1,14,22,34,35] to analyze secure information flow in software products. Leino and Joshi [22] first introduced a semantics-based approach to analyzing secure information flow based on the semantic equivalence of programs. [34,35] defined the concrete semantics of programs and lift it to an abstract domain suitable for flow analysis. In particular, they consider the domain of propositional formula representing variables' dependences. The abstract semantics is further refined by combining with numerical abstract domain which improves the precision of the analysis. A variety of logical forms are proposed to characterize information flow security. Amtoft and Banerjee [1] defined prelude semantics by treating program commands as prelude transformer. They introduced a logic based on the Abstract Interpretation of prelude semantics that makes independence between program variables explicit. They used Hoare logic and applied this logic to forward program slicing: forward l-slice is independent of h variables and is secure from information leakage. Authors in [2] defines a set of proof rules for secure information flow based on axiomatic approach. Recently, [14] proposed a model checking-based approach for reactive systems.

3   Syntax of HQL

Syntax of HQL is similar to object oriented constructs along with SQL variants through `Session` objects. The syntactic sets and the abstract syntax of HQL is depicted in Table 1. Like OOP, HQL programs are composed of a set of classes including `main` class. That is, a HQL program P is defined as $P = \langle c_{main}, \mathtt{L} \rangle$ where $c_{main} \in$ `Class` is the main class and $\mathtt{L} \subset$ `Class` are the other classes. Similarly, a class $c \in$ `Class` contains a set of fields and methods, and therefore, is defined as a triplet $c = \langle \mathtt{init}, \mathtt{F}, \mathtt{M} \rangle$, where `init` is the constructor, $\mathtt{F}$ is the set of fields, and $\mathtt{M}$ is the set of member methods.

An additional and attractive feature of HQL is the presence of `Hibernate Session` which provides a central interface between the application and Hibernate and acts as persistence manager. In HQL, an object is transient if it has just been instantiated using the new operator. Transient instances will be destroyed by the garbage collector if the application does not hold a reference anymore. A persistent instance, on the other hand, has a representation in the database and an identifier value assigned to it. Given an object, the `Hibernate Session` is used to make the object persistent. Various methods in `Hibernate Session` are used to propagate object's states from memory to the database (or vice versa).

In abstract syntax, we denote a `Session` method by a triplet $\langle \mathtt{C}, \phi, \mathtt{OP} \rangle$ where `OP` is the operation to be performed on the database tuples corresponding to a set of objects of classes $c \in \mathtt{C}$ satisfying the condition ϕ. For instance, consider the following update statement which is invoked through a session object 'ses':

```
Query Q = ses.createQuery(''UPDATE  std  SET  rank= rank+1  WHERE  mark>500'')
```

The abstract syntax of Q is denoted by

$$\langle \mathtt{C}, \phi, \mathtt{OP} \rangle = \langle \{\mathtt{std}\}, \mathtt{mark>500}, \mathtt{rank=rank+1} \rangle$$

The descriptions of `OP` in various `Session` methods are as follows:

- $\langle \mathtt{C}, \phi, \mathtt{SAVE(obj)} \rangle = \langle \{c\}, false, \mathtt{SAVE(obj)} \rangle$: Stores the state of the object `obj` in the database table t, where t corresponds to the POJO class c and `obj` is the instance of c. The pre-condition ϕ is $false$ as the method does not identify any existing tuples in the database.

Table 1. Abstract syntax of HQL `session` methods

Constants and Variables	
$n \in \mathbb{N}$	Set of Integers
$v \in \mathbb{V}$	Set of Variables
Arithmetic and Boolean Expressions	
$exp \in \mathbb{E}$	Set of Arithmetic Expressions
$exp ::= n \mid v \mid exp_1 \oplus exp_2$	
where $\oplus \in \{+, -, *, /\}$	
$b \in \mathbb{B}$	Set of Boolean Expressions
$b ::= true \mid false \mid exp_1 \otimes exp_2 \mid \neg b \mid b_1 \oslash b_2$	
where $\otimes \in \{\leq, \geq, ==, >, \neq, \dots\}$ and $\oslash \in \{\vee, \wedge\}$	
Well-formed Formulas	
$\tau \in \mathbb{T}$	Set of Terms
$\tau ::= n \mid v \mid f_n(\tau_1, \tau_2, \dots, \tau_n)$	
where f_n is an n-ary function.	
$a_f \in \mathbb{A}_f$	Set of Atomic Formulas
$a_f ::= R_n(\tau_1, \tau_2, \dots, \tau_n) \mid \tau_1 == \tau_2$	
where $R_n(\tau_1, \tau_2, \dots, \tau_n) \in \{true, false\}$	
$\phi \in \mathbb{W}$	Set of Well-formed Formulas
$\phi ::= a_f \mid \neg\phi \mid \phi_1 \oslash \phi_2$	
where $\oslash \in \{\vee, \wedge\}$	
HQL Functions	
$g(\vec{e}) ::= \texttt{GROUP BY}(e\vec{x}p) \mid id$	
where $e\vec{x}p = \langle exp_1, \dots, exp_n \mid exp_i \in \mathbb{E}\rangle$	
$r ::= \texttt{DISTINCT} \mid \texttt{ALL}$	
$s ::= \texttt{AVG} \mid \texttt{SUM} \mid \texttt{MAX} \mid \texttt{MIN} \mid \texttt{COUNT}$	
$h(exp) ::= s \circ r(exp) \mid \texttt{DISTINCT}(exp) \mid id$	
$h(*) ::= \texttt{COUNT}(*)$	
where * represents a list of database attributes denoted by $\vec{v_d}$	
$\vec{h}(\vec{x}) ::= \langle h_1(x_1), \dots, h_n(x_n)\rangle$	
where $\vec{h} = \langle h_1, \dots, h_n\rangle$ and $\vec{x} = \langle x_1, \dots, x_n \mid x_i = exp \vee x_i = *\rangle$	
$f(e\vec{x}p) ::= \texttt{ORDER BY ASC}(e\vec{x}p) \mid \texttt{ORDER BY DESC}(e\vec{x}p) \mid id$	
Session Methods	
$c \in \texttt{Class}$	Set of Classes
$c ::= \langle \texttt{init}, \texttt{F}, \texttt{M}\rangle$	
where `init` is the constructor, $\texttt{F} \subseteq \texttt{Var}$ is the	
set of fields, and `M` is the set of methods.	
$m_{ses} \in \texttt{M}_{ses}$	Set of Session methods
$m_{ses} ::= \langle \texttt{C}, \phi, \texttt{OP}\rangle$	
where $\texttt{C} \subseteq \texttt{Class}$	
$\texttt{OP} ::= \texttt{SEL}(f(e\vec{x}p'), \; r(\vec{h}(\vec{x})), \; \phi, \; g(e\vec{x}p))$	
$\mid \texttt{UPD}(\vec{v}, e\vec{x}p)$	
$\mid \texttt{SAVE(obj)}$	
$\mid \texttt{DEL}()$	
where ϕ represents 'HAVING' clause	
and `obj` denotes an instance of a class.	

- $\langle \text{C}, \phi, \text{UPD}(\vec{x}, \vec{exp}) \rangle = \langle \{c\}, \phi, \text{UPD}(\vec{v}, \vec{exp}) \rangle$: Updates the attributes corresponding to the class fields $\vec{x}$ by $\vec{exp}$ in the database table t for the tuples satisfying ϕ, where t corresponds to the POJO class c.

- $\langle \text{C}, \phi, \text{DEL}() \rangle = \langle \{c\}, \phi, \text{DEL}() \rangle$: Deletes the tuples satisfying ϕ in t, where t is the database table corresponding to the POJO class c.

- $\langle \text{C}, \phi, \text{SEL}\big(f(\vec{exp'}),\ r(\vec{h}(\vec{x})),\ \phi',\ g(\vec{exp})\big) \rangle$: Selects information from the database tables corresponding to the set of POJO classes C, and returns the equivalent representations in the form of objects.

It is immediate that in case of SAVE() the condition ϕ is *false* and C is singleton set $\{c\}$. As UPD() and DEL() always target single class, the set C is also singleton $\{c\}$ in those cases. However, C may not be singleton in case of SEL().

4   Concrete Semantics of HQL

In this section, we define the semantics of HQL by (i) extending the OOP semantics [25] and (ii) defining the semantics of Session methods in terms of the semantics of database query languages [17].

4.1   Concrete Semantics of OOP [25]

Let Var, Val and Loc be the set of variables, the domain of values and the set of memory locations respectively. The set of environments, stores and states are defined below:

- The set of environments is defined as Env : Var $\longrightarrow$ Loc
- The set of stores is defined as Store : Loc $\longrightarrow$ Val
- The set of states is defined as Σ : Env × Store. So, a state $\rho \in \Sigma$ is denoted by a tuple $\langle e, s \rangle$ where $e \in$ Env and $s \in$ Store.

Some special variables (pc, V_{in}, V_{out}) are used in the subsequent part which represent the following: (i) $\rho(pc)$ is the program counter; (ii) $\rho(V_{in})$ is the input value of the current method; (iii) $\rho(V_{out})$ is the value returned by the current method.

Constructor and Method Semantics. During object creation, the class constructor is invoked and object fields are instantiated by input values. Given a store s, the constructor maps its fields to fresh locations and then assigns values into those locations. Constructor never returns any output.

Definition 1 (Constructor Semantics). *Given a store s. Let $\{a_{in}, a_{pc}\} \subseteq$ Loc be the free locations, $Val_{in} \subseteq Val$ be the semantic domain for input values. Let $v_{in} \in Val_{in}$ and pc_{exit} be the input value and the exit point of the constructor.*

Table 2. An example class

```
1.    class Demo {
2.        int k;
3.        Demo(int i) {
4.            k = i;
5.        }
6.        int even() {
7.            if(k % 2 == 0)
8.                return 1;
9.            else return 0;
10.       }
11.       int * mul ( int j ) {
12.           k = k * j;
13.           return &k;
14.       }
15. }
```

The semantic of the class constructor $init$, $S[\![init]\!] \in (\textbf{Store} \times \textbf{Val} \rightarrow \wp(\textbf{Env} \times \textbf{Store}))$, is defined by

$$S[\![init]\!](s, v_{in}) = \{(e_0, s_0) \mid (e_0 \triangleq V_{in} \rightarrow a_{in}, pc \rightarrow a_{pc}) \wedge (s_0 \triangleq s[a_{in} \rightarrow v_{in}, a_{pc} \rightarrow pc_{exit}])\}$$

Definition 2 (Method Semantics). Let $\textbf{Val}_{in} \subseteq \textbf{Val}$ and $\textbf{Val}_{out} \subseteq \textbf{Val}$ be the semantic domains for the input values and the output values respectively. Let $v_{in} \in \textbf{Val}_{in}$ be the input values, a_{in} and a_{pc} be the fresh memory locations, and pc_{exit} be the exit point of the method m. The semantic of a method m, $S[\![m]\!] \in (\textbf{Env} \times \textbf{Store} \times \textbf{Val}_{in} \rightarrow \wp(\textbf{Store} \times \textbf{Env} \times \textbf{Val}_{out}))$, is defined as

$$S[\![m]\!](e, s, v_{in}) = \{(e', s', v_{out}) \mid (e' \triangleq e[V_{in} \rightarrow a_{in}, pc \rightarrow a_{pc}]) \wedge$$
$$(s' \triangleq s[a_{in} \rightarrow v_{in}, a_{pc} \rightarrow pc_{exit}]) \wedge v_{out} \in \textbf{Val}_{out}\}$$

Example 1. Consider the example of Table 2. The class constructor Demo() creates a new environment consists of field k. The semantics of constructor Demo() and the semantics of the methods even() and mul() are defined below:

$$S[\![\text{Demo()}]\!](s, i) = \{(e_0, s_0) \mid (e_0 \triangleq k \rightarrow a_{in}, pc \rightarrow a_{pc}) \wedge (s_0 \triangleq s[a_{in} \rightarrow i, a_{pc} \rightarrow 5])\}$$

$$S[\![\text{even()}]\!](e, s, \varnothing) = \{(e, s', v_{out}) \mid (s' \triangleq s[e(pc) \rightarrow 10]) \wedge (v_{out} = \text{if}(s(e(k))\%2)\ ?1 : 0)\}$$

$$S[\![\text{mul()}]\!](e, s, j) = \{(e, s', v_{out}) \mid (s' \triangleq s[e(k) \rightarrow s(e(k)) * j, e(pc) \rightarrow 14]) \wedge v_{out} = e(k)\}$$

Observe that even() takes no input and returns an integer value as output, whereas mul() takes an integer value as input and returns an address as output.

Object and Class Semantics. Object semantics is defined in terms of inter-action history between the program-context and the object. A direct interaction takes place when the program-context calls any member-method of the object, whereas an indirect interaction occurs when the program-context updates any address escaped from the object's scope. However, both direct or indirect inter-action can cause a change in an interaction state (see Definition 3).

Definition 3 (Interaction States). *The set of interaction states is defined by*

$$\Sigma = \textbf{Env} \times \textbf{Store} \times \textbf{Val}_{out} \times \wp(\textbf{Loc})$$

where $\textbf{Env}$, $\textbf{Store}$, $\textbf{Val}_{out}$, *and* $\textbf{Loc}$ *are the set of application environments, the set of stores, the set of output values, and the set of addresses respectively.*

Definition 4 (Initial Interaction States). *Let* $v_{in} \in \textbf{Val}_{in}$ *be an input to the class constructor* $\textbf{init}$ *when creating an object. Let* $s \in \textbf{Store}$ *be a store. Then the set of initial interaction states is defined by*

$$\mathcal{I}_0 = \big\{\langle e_0, s_0, \phi, \emptyset \rangle \mid S[\![\textbf{init}]\!](v_{in}, s) \ni \langle e_0, s_0 \rangle \big\}$$

Observe that ϕ denotes no output produced by the constructor and $\emptyset$ represents the empty context with no escaped address.

Example 2 (Initial Interaction States). Consider the example of Table 2. The input to the constructor is i. Given a store s, the initial interaction states are

$$\mathcal{I}_0 = \big\{\langle e_0, s_0, \phi, \emptyset \rangle \mid S[\![\texttt{Sample()}]\!](i, s) \ni \langle e_0, s_0 \rangle \big\}$$
$$= \big\{\langle e_0, s_0, \phi, \emptyset \rangle \mid (e_0 \triangleq a \rightarrow a_{in}, pc \rightarrow a_{pc}) \wedge (s_0 \triangleq s[a_{in} \rightarrow i, a_{pc} \rightarrow 5]) \big\}$$

Observe that the third element in an initial state is ϕ because constructor does not return any value as output. Similarly the fourth element is $\emptyset$ because no address is escaped from the object's scope after execution of $\texttt{sample()}$.

Transition Relation. Let $\texttt{Lab} = (\mathbb{M} \times \textbf{Val}_{in}) \cup \{\textbf{upd}\}$ be a set of labels, where $\mathbb{M}$ is the set of class-methods, $\textbf{Val}_{in}$ is the set of input values and $\textbf{upd}$ denotes an indirect update operation by the context. The transition relation $\mathcal{T} : \Sigma \rightarrow \wp(\Sigma \times \texttt{Lab})$ specifies which successor interaction states $\sigma' = \langle e', s', v', \textbf{Esc}' \rangle \in \Sigma$ can follow

1. when an object's methods $m \in \mathbb{M}$ with input $v_{in} \in \textbf{Val}_{in}$ is directly invoked on an interaction state $\sigma = \langle e, s, v, \textbf{Esc} \rangle$ (**direct interaction**), or
2. the context indirectly updates an address escaped from an object's scope (**indirect interaction**).

Definition 5 (Direct Interaction $\mathcal{T}_{dir}$). *Transition on Direct Interaction is defined below:*

$$\mathcal{T}_{dir}(\langle e, s, v, \textbf{Esc} \rangle) = \big\{ \big(\langle e', s', v', \textbf{Esc}' \rangle, (m, v_{in})\big) \mid S[\![m]\!](\langle e, s, v_{in} \rangle) \ni \langle e', s', v' \rangle$$
$$\wedge\ \textbf{Esc}' = \textbf{Esc} \cup \textbf{reach}(v', s') \big\}$$

where

$$reach(v,s) = \begin{cases} if\ v \in Loc \\ \quad \{v\} \cup \{reach(e'(f),s) \mid \exists B.\ B = \{init, F, M\},\ f \in F, \\ \quad s(v)\ is\ an\ instance\ of\ B,\ s(s(v)) = e' \\ else\ \emptyset \end{cases}$$

Example 3 (Direct interaction $\mathscr{T}_{dir}$). Consider the example of Table 2. The context can invoke any one of the two methods of Sample class. Therefore given an interaction state $\sigma = \langle e, s, v, \text{Esc}\rangle$, the set of successor interaction states are

$$\mathscr{T}_{dir}(\langle e,s,v,\text{Esc}\rangle) = \{(\langle e,s',v',\text{Esc}\rangle, (\texttt{parity}(),\phi)) \mid S[\![\texttt{parity}()]\!](\langle e,s,\phi\rangle) \ni \langle e,s',v'\rangle\}$$

$$\bigcup \{(\langle e,s',v',\text{Esc}'\rangle, (\texttt{incr}(),j)) \mid S[\![\texttt{incr}()]\!](\langle e,s,j\rangle) \ni \langle e,s',v'\rangle$$

$$\wedge \text{Esc}' = \text{Esc} \cup \{v'\}\}$$

Definition 6 (Indirect Interaction $\mathscr{T}_{ind}$). *Transition on Indirect Interaction is defined below:*

$$\mathscr{T}_{ind}(\langle e,s,v,\text{Esc}\rangle) = \{(\langle e,s',v,\text{Esc}\rangle, \textbf{upd}) \mid \exists a \in \text{Esc}.\ \textit{Update}(a,s) \ni s'\}$$

where $\textit{Update}(a,s) = \{s' \mid \exists v \in \textbf{Val}.\ s' = s[a \leftarrow v]\}$

Definition 7 (Transition Relation $\mathscr{T}$). *Let $\sigma \in \Sigma$ be an interaction state. The transition relation $\mathscr{T} : \Sigma \rightarrow \wp(\Sigma \times \textbf{Lab})$ is defined as $\mathscr{T} = \mathscr{T}_{dir} \cup \mathscr{T}_{ind}$, where $\mathscr{T}_{dir}$ and $\mathscr{T}_{ind}$ represent direct and indirect transitions respectively.*

Let us denote a transition between interaction states σ_1 and σ_2 by $\sigma_1 \xrightarrow{\ell} \sigma_2$ where $\ell \in \textbf{Lab}$.

Objects Fix-point Semantics. Given a store $s \in \textbf{Store}$, the set of initial interaction states is defined as

$$\mathcal{I}_0 = \{\langle e_0, s_0, \phi, \emptyset\rangle \mid S[\![\texttt{init}]\!](v_{in},s) \ni \langle e_0, s_0\rangle, v_{in} \in \textbf{Val}_{in}\}$$

The fix-point trace semantics of obj, according to [12], is defined as

$$\mathscr{T}[\![\texttt{obj}]\!](\mathcal{I}_0) = \text{lfp}_{\emptyset}^{\subseteq} \mathcal{F}(\mathcal{I}_0) = \bigcup_{i \leq \omega} \mathcal{F}^i(\mathcal{I}_0)$$

where $\mathcal{F}(\mathcal{I}) = \lambda T.\ \mathcal{I} \cup \{\sigma_0 \xrightarrow{\ell_0} \dots \xrightarrow{\ell_{n-1}} \sigma_n \xrightarrow{\ell_n} \sigma_{n+1} \mid \sigma_0 \xrightarrow{\ell_0} \dots \xrightarrow{\ell_{n-1}} \sigma_n \in T \wedge$
$$(\sigma_{n+1}, \ell_n) \in \mathscr{T}(\sigma_n)\}$$

Class Semantics. A class is nothing but a description of the set of objects. The semantics of a class c is defined as

$$S[\![\texttt{c}]\!] = \cup \{\mathscr{T}[\![\texttt{obj}]\!](\mathcal{I}_0) \mid \text{``obj'' is an instance of a class c and } \mathcal{I}_0 \text{ is the}$$
$$\text{set of initial interaction states}\}$$

Observe that the semantic definitions of objects and classes aim at verifying invariance properties of classes.

Object-Oriented Program Semantics. Let $P = \langle c_{main}, L \rangle$ be an object-oriented program. Let $\rightarrow \subseteq (\mathbf{Env} \times \mathbf{Store}) \times (\mathbf{Env} \times \mathbf{Store})$ be a transition relation and $S_0 \in \wp(\mathbf{Env} \times \mathbf{Store})$ be a set of initial states such that $\forall \rho_0 \in S_0$. $\rho_0(currentMethod) = c_{main}$ and $\rho_0(pc) = pc_{main}$ where pc_{main} is the entry point of main method in c_{main}. The semantic of P is defined as

$$S[\![P]\!](S_0) = \mathrm{lfp}_{\emptyset}^{\subseteq} \lambda X. \ S_0 \cup \{\rho_0 \rightarrow \rho_1 \rightarrow \cdots \rightarrow \rho_n \rightarrow \rho_{n+1} \mid \rho_{n+1} \in (\mathbf{Env} \times \mathbf{Store}) \wedge$$
$$\rho_0 \rightarrow \rho_1 \rightarrow \cdots \rightarrow \rho_n \in X \wedge \rho_n \rightarrow \rho_{n+1}\}$$

4.2 Concrete Semantics of HQL

In order to define the semantics of HQL, let us recall the notion of database environment ρ_d and table environment ρ_t from [17].

Database Environment. We consider a database as a set of indexed tables $\{t_i \mid i \in I_x\}$ for a given set of indexes I_x. We define database environment by a function ρ_d whose domain is I_x, such that for $i \in I_x$, $\rho_d(i) = t_i$.

Table Environment. Given a database environment ρ_d and a table $t \in d$. We define $attr(t) = \{a_1, a_2, ..., a_k\}$. So, $t \subseteq D_1 \times D_2 \times .... \times D_k$ where, a_i is the attribute corresponding to the typed domain D_i. A table environment ρ_t for a table t is defined as a function such that for any attribute $a_i \in attr(t)$,

$$\rho_t(a_i) = \langle \pi_i(l_j) \mid l_j \in t \rangle$$

where π is the projection operator, *i.e.* $\pi_i(l_j)$ is the ith element of the l_j-th row. In other words, ρ_t maps a_i to the ordered set of values over the rows of the table t.

Interaction State. We extend the notion of interaction states of OOP to the case of HQL, considering the interaction of context with **Session** objects. To this aim, we include database environment in the definition of HQL states. The set of interaction states of HQL is, thus, defined by

$$\Sigma = \mathbf{Env} \times \mathbf{Store} \times \mathfrak{E}_d \times \mathbf{Val}_{out} \times \wp(\mathbf{Loc})$$

where **Env**, **Store**, $\mathfrak{E}_d$, **Val**$_{out}$, and **Loc** are the set of application environments, the set of stores, the set of database environments, the set of output values, and the set of addresses respectively.

The set of initial interaction states of HQL is defined by

$$\mathcal{I}_0 = \{\langle e_0, s_0, \rho_{d_0}, \phi, \emptyset \rangle \mid S[\![\mathtt{init}]\!](v_{in}, s) \ni \langle e_0, s_0 \rangle\}$$

where $v_{in} \in \mathbf{Val}_{in}$ is an input to the class constructor **init** when creating an object and $s \in \mathbf{Store}$ is a store. ρ_{d_0} is the initial database environment.

The semantics of conventional constructors, methods, objects, classes in HQL are defined in the same way as in the case of OOP. The **Session** methods require an 'ad-hoc' treatment. We define its concrete semantics by specifying how the methods are executed on (e, s, ρ_d) where $e \in \texttt{Env}$ is an environment, $s \in \texttt{Store}$ is a store, and $\rho_d \in \mathfrak{E}_d$ is a database environment, resulting into new state $(e', s', \rho_{d'})$. The semantic definitions are expressed in terms of the semantics of database statements $\texttt{SELECT}, \texttt{INSERT}, \texttt{UPDATE}, \texttt{DELETE}$ [17].

We use the following functions in the subsequent part: $map(v)$ maps v to the underlying database object; $var(exp)$ returns the variables appearing in exp; $attr(t)$ returns the attributes associated with table t; $dom(f)$ returns the domain of f.

The semantic function is defined as:

$$S[\![(\texttt{C}, \phi, \texttt{op})]\!](e, s, \rho_d)$$

$$= \begin{cases} S[\![(\texttt{C}, \phi, \texttt{op})]\!](e, s, \rho_{t'}) \text{ if } \exists t_1, \ldots, t_n \in dom(\rho_d): \ \texttt{C} = \{c_1, \ldots, c_n\} \\ \qquad\qquad\qquad \wedge (\forall i \in [1 \ldots n]. \ t_i = map(c_i)) \wedge t' = t_1 \times t_2 \times \cdots \times t_n. \\ \\ \bot \quad otherwise. \end{cases}$$

Semantics of Session Method UPD(). Consider the Session method $\langle\{c\}, \phi, \texttt{UPD}(\vec{v}, \vec{exp})\rangle$. The semantics is defined below[2]:

$$S[\![\langle\{c\}, \phi, \texttt{UPD}(\vec{v}, \vec{exp})\rangle]\!]$$

$$= \lambda(e, s, \rho_t). \text{ let } c = \langle \texttt{init}, \texttt{F}, \texttt{M}\rangle \text{ such that } map(\texttt{F}) = attr(t) \text{ and } map(\vec{v}) = \vec{a} \subseteq attr(t)$$
$$\text{where } \vec{v} \subseteq \texttt{F}, \text{ and let } \phi_d = \texttt{PE}[\![\phi]\!](e, s, \texttt{F}) \text{ and } \vec{exp}_d = \texttt{PE}[\![\vec{exp}]\!](e, s, \texttt{F}) \text{ in}$$
$$\{\langle e, s, \rho_{t'}\rangle \mid \rho_{t'} \in S[\![\langle \texttt{UPDATE}(\vec{a}, \vec{exp}_d), \phi_d\rangle]\!](\rho_t)\}.$$

The auxiliary function $\texttt{PE}[\![X]\!]$ (which stands for partial evaluation) is used in the definition above to convert variables in X into the corresponding database objects. This is defined by

$$\texttt{PE}[\![X]\!](e, s, \texttt{F}) = X'$$

where $X' = X[x_i/v_i]$ for all $v_i \in var(X)$ and $x_i = \begin{cases} map(v_i) & \text{if } v_i \in \texttt{F} \\ \\ E[\![v_i]\!](e, s) & \text{otherwise} \end{cases}$

Example 4. Let us consider a POJO class std which corresponds to the database table t_1 depicted in Table 3(a). Consider the following HQL code:

Query $Q = ses.\texttt{createQuery}("\texttt{UPDATE std SET} \ rank = rank + 1, \ mark$
$= mark - 50 \times 2 \ \texttt{WHERE} \ mark > 500");$
int $R = Q.\texttt{executeUpdate}();$

---

[2] Observe that, for the sake of simplicity, we do not consider here the method REFRESH() which synchronize the in-memory objects state with that of the underlying database.

Table 3. After execution of the UPDATE operation

(a) Table t_1

tsid	tmark	trank	tdno
1	800	5	3
2	400	10	2
3	600	7	3
4	1000	1	1

(b) Table t_2: After Updation

tsid	tmark	trank	tdno
1	700	6	3
2	400	10	2
3	500	8	3
4	900	2	1

The abstract syntax of the Session method above is $\langle\{c\}, \phi, \text{UPD}(\vec{v}, \vec{exp})\rangle$, where

- $\{c\} = \{\text{std}\}$,
- $\phi = $ "$mark > 500$",
- $\text{UPD}(\vec{v}, \vec{exp}) = \text{UPD}(\langle rank, mark\rangle, \langle rank + 1, mark - 50 \times 2\rangle)$

Given the table environment ρ_{t_1} in Table 3(a), the semantics is defined as:

$$S[\![\langle\{\text{std}\}, (mark > 500), \text{UPD}(\langle rank, mark\rangle, \langle rank + 1, mark - 50 \times 2\rangle)\rangle]\!]$$

$$=\lambda(e, s, \rho_{t_1}). \text{ let } \text{std} = \langle\text{std}(), F, M\rangle \text{ such that } F = \langle sid, mark, rank, dno\rangle \text{ and}$$
$$map(F) = attr(t) = \langle tsid, tmark, trank, tdno\rangle \text{ and}$$
$$map(\vec{v}) = map(\langle rank, mark\rangle) = \langle trank, tmark\rangle \subseteq attr(t), \text{ and let}$$
$$(tmark > 500) = PE[\![(\text{std}.mark > 500)]\!](e, s, F) \text{ and}$$
$$\langle trank + 1, tmark - 50 \times 2\rangle = PE[\![\langle rank + 1, mark - 50 \times 2\rangle]\!](e, s, F) \text{ in}$$
$$\{\langle e, s, \rho_{t_2}\rangle \mid \rho_{t_2} \in S[\![\langle\text{UPDATE}(\langle trank, tmark\rangle, \langle trank + 1, tmark - 50 \times 2\rangle),$$
$$(tmark > 500)\rangle]\!](\rho_{t_1})\}.$$

The resulting table environment ρ_{t_2} in shown in Table 3(b). The semantics of other Session methods are in Table 4.

Fix-Point Semantics of HQL. Let us define transition relation, considering nondeterministic executions, as $\mathscr{T} : M_{ses} \times \Sigma \to \wp(\Sigma)$. This specifies which successor interaction states $\sigma' = \langle e', s', \rho_{d'},\rangle \in \Sigma$ can follow when a Session method $m_{ses} = \langle C, \phi, \text{op}\rangle \in M_{ses}$ is invoked on an interaction state $\sigma = \langle e, s, \rho_d\rangle$. That is,

$$\mathscr{T}_{ses}[\![m_{ses}]\!](\langle e, s, \rho_d\rangle) = \{(\langle e', s', \rho_{d'}\rangle) \mid S[\![m_{ses}]\!](\langle e, s, \rho_d\rangle) \ni \langle e', s', \rho_{d'}\rangle \wedge m_{ses} \in M_{ses}\}$$

We now define the transition relation, by considering (i) the direct interaction, when a conventional method is directly invoked, (ii) the session interaction, when a Session method is invoked, and (iii) the indirect transition, when context updates any address escaped from the object's scope.

Definition 8 (Transition Relation $\mathscr{T}$). *Let $\sigma \in \Sigma$ be an interaction state. The transition relation $\mathscr{T} : \text{Lab} \times \Sigma \to \wp(\Sigma)$ is defined as $\mathscr{T} = \mathscr{T}_{dir} \cup \mathscr{T}_{ind} \cup \mathscr{T}_{ses}$, where $\mathscr{T}_{dir}$, $\mathscr{T}_{ind}$ and $\mathscr{T}_{ses}$ represent direct, indirect, and session transitions respectively. Lab represents the set of labels which include Session methods M_{ses}, conventional class methods $\mathbb{M}$, and an indirect update operation Upd by the context.*

Table 4. Semantics of `Session` methods

The semantics of Session method $\langle \{c\}, \phi, \texttt{SAVE(obj)} \rangle$:

$S[\![\langle \{c\}, \phi, \texttt{SAVE(obj)} \rangle]\!]$
$= S[\![\langle \{c\}, \textit{false}, \texttt{SAVE(obj)} \rangle]\!]$
$= \lambda(e, s, \rho_t).$ let $c = \langle \texttt{init}, F, M \rangle$ such that $map(F) = attr(t) = \vec{a}$, and let
$\quad s(e(\texttt{obj})) = e'$ such that $s(e'(F)) = \vec{val}$, in
$\quad \{\langle e, s, \rho_{t'} \rangle \mid \rho_{t'} \in S[\![\langle \texttt{INSERT}(\vec{a}, \vec{val}), \textit{false} \rangle]\!](\rho_t)\}.$

The semantics of Session method $\langle \{c\}, \phi, \texttt{DEL()} \rangle$:

$S[\![\langle \{c\}, \phi, \texttt{DEL()} \rangle]\!]$
$= \lambda(e, s, \rho_t).$ let $c = \langle \texttt{init}, F, M \rangle$ such that $map(F) = attr(t) = \vec{a}$ and let $\phi_d = PE[\![\phi]\!](e, s, F)$
$\quad$ in $\{\langle e, s, \rho_{t'} \rangle \mid \rho_{t'} \in S[\![\langle \texttt{DELETE}(\vec{a}), \phi_d \rangle]\!](\rho_t)\}$

The semantics of $\langle C, \phi, \texttt{SEL}(f(\vec{exp}'), r(\vec{h}(\vec{x})), \phi', g(\vec{exp})) \rangle$:

$S[\![\langle C, \phi, \texttt{SEL}(f(\vec{exp}'), r(\vec{h}(\vec{x})), \phi', g(\vec{exp})) \rangle]\!]$
$= \lambda(e, s, \rho_t).$ let $C = \{\langle \texttt{init}_i, F_i, M_i \rangle \mid i = 1, \ldots, n\}$, and $F = \bigcup_{i=1,\ldots,n} F_i$, and
$\quad \langle \vec{exp}'_d, \vec{x}_d, \phi'_d, \vec{exp}_d, \phi_d \rangle = PE[\![\langle \vec{exp}', \vec{x}, \phi', \vec{exp}, \phi \rangle]\!](e, s, F)$, and let
$\quad \rho_{t'} = S[\![\langle \texttt{SELECT}(f(\vec{exp}'_d), r(\vec{h}(\vec{x}_d)), \phi'_d, g(\vec{exp}_d)), \phi_d \rangle]\!](\rho_t)$ and
$\quad (e', s') = \bigsqcup_{\forall l_i \in t'} S[\![\texttt{Object()}]\!](s, val(l_i))$ in $\{\langle e', s', \rho_t \rangle\}.$

Observe that $\texttt{val}(l_i)$ converts each tuple $l_i \in t'$ into input values, and $S[\![\texttt{Object()}]\!](s, \texttt{val}(l_i))$ invokes the object constructor `Object()` which creates an object by initializing the fields with $\texttt{val}(l_i)$. This is done for all tuples $l_i \in t'$, resulting into new (e', s').

We denote a transition by $\sigma \xrightarrow{a} \sigma'$ when application of a label $a \in \texttt{Lab}$ on interaction state σ results into a new state σ'.

Let $\mathcal{I}_0$ be the set of initial interaction states. The fix-point trace semantics of HQL program P is defined as

$$\mathscr{T}[\![P]\!](\mathcal{I}_0) = \text{lfp}_{\emptyset}^{\subseteq} \mathcal{F}(\mathcal{I}_0) = \bigcup_{i \leq \omega} \mathcal{F}^i(\mathcal{I}_0)$$

where $\mathcal{F}(\mathcal{I}) = \lambda T.\ \mathcal{I} \cup \left\{ \sigma_0 \xrightarrow{a_0} \ldots \xrightarrow{a_{n-1}} \sigma_n \xrightarrow{a_n} \sigma_{n+1} \mid \sigma_0 \xrightarrow{a_0} \ldots \xrightarrow{a_{n-1}} \sigma_n \in T \right.$
$\left. \wedge \sigma_n \xrightarrow{a_n} \sigma_{n+1} \in \mathscr{T} \right\}$

5   Abstract Semantics of HQL

Abstract interpretation [11,12] provides a general theoretical foundation to specify static analyses, to guarantee their correctness, to tune their precision according to efficiency issues, and to compare and to combine them in a modular way. It allows to deal separately with concerns that typically interleave, including fix-point algorithms, abstract domains, and termination criteria handled by widening operators. Its theoretical and practical impact has been demonstrated in various application fields, in particular for safety and security analysis.

In [34,35], authors used the Abstract Interpretation framework to define an abstract semantics of imperative languages using symbolic domain of positive propositional formulae in the form

$$\bigwedge_{0\leq i\leq n,\ 0\leq j\leq m} \{y_i \rightarrow z_j\}$$

which means that the values of variable z_j possibly depend on the values of variable y_i. Later, [18] extends this to the case of structured query languages. The computation of abstract semantics of a program in the propositional formulae domain provides a sound approximation of variable dependences, which allows to capture possible information flow in the program. The information leakage analysis is then performed by checking the satisfiability of formulae after assigning truth values to variables based on their sensitivity levels.

Let Pos and $\mathbb{L}$ be the domain of propositional formulae and the set of program points respectively. An abstract state $\sigma^\sharp \in \Sigma^\sharp \equiv \mathbb{L} \times$ Pos is a pair $\langle \ell, \psi \rangle$ where $\psi \in$ Pos represents the variable dependences, in the form of propositional formulae, among program variables up to the program label $\ell \in \mathbb{L}$.

Methods in HQL include a set of imperative statements[3]. We assume, for the sake of the simplicity, that attackers are able to observe public variables inside of the main method only. Therefore, our analysis only aims at identifying variable dependences at input-output labels of methods.

The abstract transition semantics of constructors and conventional methods are defined below.

Definition 9 (Abstract Transition Semantics of Constructor). *Consider a class* $c = \langle init, F, M \rangle$ *where* $init$ *is a default constructor. Let* ℓ *be the label of* $init$. *The abstract transition semantics of* $init$ *is defined as*

$$\mathcal{T}^\sharp[\![^\ell init]\!] = \{(\ell, \psi) \rightarrow (Succ(^\ell init), \psi)\}$$

where $Succ(^\ell init)$ *denotes the successor label of* $init$. *Observe that the default constructor is used to initialize the objects-fields only, and it does not add any new dependence.*

The abstract transition semantics of parameterized constructors are defined in the same way as of class methods $m \in M$.

Definition 10 (Abstract Transition Semantics of Methods). *Let* $U \in \wp(Var)$ *be the set of variables which are passed as actual parameters when invoked a method* $m \in M$ *on an abstract state* (ℓ, ψ) *at program label* ℓ. *Let* $V \in \wp(Var)$ *be*

---

[3] For a detailed abstract transition semantics of imperative statements, see [34].

the formal arguments in the definition of m. We assume that $U \cap V = \emptyset$. Let a and b be the variable returned by m and the variable to which the value returned by m is assigned. The abstract transition semantics is defined as

$$\mathscr{T}^{\sharp}[\![^{\ell}m]\!] = \{(\ell, \psi) \rightarrow (\textbf{Succ}(^{\ell}m), \psi')\}$$

where $\psi' = \{x_i \rightarrow y_i \mid x_i \in U, y_i \in V\} \cup \{a \rightarrow b\} \cup \psi$ and $\textbf{Succ}(^{\ell}m)$ is the label of the successor of m.

Let us classify the high-level HQL variables into two distinct sets: $\textsf{Var}_d$ and $\textsf{Var}_a$. The variables which have a correspondence with database attributes belong to the set $\textsf{Var}_d$. Otherwise, the variables are treated as usual variables and belong to $\textsf{Var}_a$. We denote variables in $\textsf{Var}_d$ by the notation $\bar{v}$, in order to differentiate them from the variables in $\textsf{Var}_a$. This leads to four types of dependences which may arise in HQL programs: $x \rightarrow y$, $\bar{x} \rightarrow y$, $x \rightarrow \bar{y}$ and $\bar{x} \rightarrow \bar{y}$, where $x, y \in \textsf{Var}_a$ and $\bar{x}, \bar{y} \in \textsf{Var}_d$.

Definition of Abstract Transition Function $\mathscr{T}^{\sharp}$ **for** $\textsf{Session}$ **methods.** The abstract labeled transition semantics of various $\textsf{Session}$ methods are defined below, where by $\textsf{Var}(exp)$ and $\textsf{Field}(c)$ we denote the set of variables in exp and the set of class-fields in the class c respectively. The function $\textsf{Map}(v)$ is defined as:

$$\textsf{Map}(v) = \begin{cases} \bar{v} \text{ if } v \text{ has correspondence with a database attribute,} \\ v \text{ otherwise.} \end{cases}$$

Notice that in the definition of $\mathscr{T}^{\sharp}$ the notation $\tilde{v}$ stands for either v or $\bar{v}$. Let $\textsf{SF}(\psi)$ denotes the set of subformulas in ψ, and the operator $\ominus$ is defined by $\psi_1 \ominus \psi_2 = \bigwedge (\textsf{SF}(\psi_1) \backslash \textsf{SF}(\psi_2))$.

The transition semantics for Session method m_{save}

$\mathscr{T}^{\sharp}[\![^{\ell}m_{save}]\!]$
$\overset{def}{=} \mathscr{T}^{\sharp}[\![^{\ell}(\textsf{C}, \phi, \textsf{SAVE(obj)})]\!]$
$\overset{def}{=} \mathscr{T}^{\sharp}[\![^{\ell}(\{c\}, \textsf{FALSE}, \textsf{SAVE(obj)})]\!]$
$\overset{def}{=} \{\langle \ell, \psi \rangle \xrightarrow{\textsf{SAVE}} \langle \textbf{Succ}(^{\ell}m_{save}), \psi \rangle\}$

The transition semantics for Session method m_{upd}

$\mathscr{T}^{\sharp}[\![^{\ell}m_{upd}]\!]$
$\overset{def}{=} \mathscr{T}^{\sharp}[\![^{\ell}(\textsf{C}, \phi, \textsf{UPD}(\bar{v}, e\vec{x}p))]\!]$
$\overset{def}{=} \mathscr{T}^{\sharp}[\![^{\ell}(\{c\}, \phi, \textsf{UPD}(\bar{v}, e\vec{x}p))]\!]$
$\overset{def}{=} \{\langle \ell, \psi \rangle \xrightarrow{\textsf{UPD}} \langle \textbf{Succ}(^{\ell}m_{upd}), \psi' \rangle\}$
where $\psi' = \bigwedge \{\tilde{y} \rightarrow \bar{z}_i \mid y \in \textsf{Var}[\![\phi]\!], \tilde{y} = \textsf{Map}(y), \bar{z}_i \in \bar{v}\} \bigcup$

$\bigwedge \{\widetilde{y_i} \to \overline{z_i} \mid y_i \in \mathtt{Var}[\![exp_i]\!], exp_i \in e\vec{x}p, \widetilde{y_i} = \mathtt{Map}(y_i), \overline{z_i} \in \vec{v}\} \bigcup \psi''$

and $\psi'' = \begin{cases} \psi \ominus (\widetilde{a} \to \overline{z_i} \mid \overline{z_i} \in \vec{v} \wedge a \in \mathtt{Var} \wedge \widetilde{a} = \mathtt{Map}(a)) & \text{if } \phi \text{ is } \mathtt{TRUE} \text{ by default.} \\ \psi & \text{otherwise} \end{cases}$

The transition semantics for Session method m_{del}

$\mathcal{T}^{\#}[\![^\ell m_{del}]\!]$

$\stackrel{def}{=} \mathcal{T}^{\#}[\![^\ell(\mathtt{C}, \phi, \mathtt{DEL}())]\!]$

$\stackrel{def}{=} \mathcal{T}^{\#}[\![^\ell(\{c\}, \phi, \mathtt{DEL}())]\!]$

$\stackrel{def}{=} \{\langle \ell, \psi \rangle \xrightarrow{\mathtt{DEL}} \langle \mathtt{Succ}(^\ell m_{del}), \psi' \rangle\}$

where $\psi' = \bigwedge \{\widetilde{y} \to \overline{z} \mid y \in \mathtt{Var}[\![\phi]\!], \widetilde{y} = \mathtt{Map}(y), \overline{z} \in \mathtt{Field}(c)\} \bigcup \psi''$

and $\psi'' = \begin{cases} \psi \ominus (\widetilde{a} \to \overline{z_i} \mid \overline{z_i} \in \vec{v} \wedge a \in \mathtt{Var} \wedge \widetilde{a} = \mathtt{Map}(a)) & \text{if } \phi \text{ is } \mathtt{TRUE} \text{ by default.} \\ \psi & \text{otherwise} \end{cases}$

The transition semantics for Session method m_{sel}

$\mathcal{T}^{\#}[\![^\ell m_{sel}]\!]$

$\stackrel{def}{=} \mathcal{T}^{\#}[\![^\ell(\mathtt{C}, \phi, \mathtt{SEL}(f(e\vec{x}p'), \ r(\vec{h}(\vec{x})), \ \phi, \ g(e\vec{x}p)))]\!]$

$\stackrel{def}{=} \{\langle \ell, \psi \rangle \xrightarrow{\mathtt{SEL}} \langle \mathtt{Succ}(^\ell m_{sel}), \psi' \rangle\}$

where $\psi' = \bigwedge \{\widetilde{y} \to \widetilde{z} \mid y \in (\mathtt{Var}[\![\phi]\!] \cup \mathtt{Var}[\![\vec{e}]\!] \cup \mathtt{Var}[\![\phi']\!] \cup \mathtt{Var}[\![\vec{e'}]\!]), z \in \mathtt{Var}[\![\vec{x}]\!],$
$\widetilde{y} = \mathtt{Map}(y), \widetilde{z} = \mathtt{Map}(z)\} \bigcup \psi$

6   Information Leakage Analysis

We are now in position to use the abstract semantics defined in the previous section to identify possible sensitive database information leakage through high-level HQL variables. After obtaining over-approximation of variable dependences at each program point, we assign truth values to each variable based on their sensitivity level, and we check the satisfiability of propositional formulae representing variable dependences [34].

Since our main objective is to identify the leakage of sensitive database information possibly due to the interaction of high-level variables, we assume, according to the policy, that different security classes are assigned to database attributes. Accordingly, we assign security levels to the variables in $\mathtt{Var}_d$ based on the correspondences. Similarly, we assign the security levels of the variables in $\mathtt{Var}_a$ based on their use in the program. For instance, the variables which are used on output channels, are considered as public variables. Observe that for the variables with unknown security class, it may be computed based on the dependence of it on the other application variables or database attributes of known security classes.

Let $\Gamma : \mathtt{Var} \to \{L, H, N\}$ be a function that assigns to each of the variables a security class, either public (L) or private (H) or unknown (N).

After computing abstract semantics of HQL program P, the security class of variables with unknown level (N) in P are upgraded to either H or L, according to the following function:

$$\text{Upgrade}(v) = Z \text{ if } \exists\, (u \to v) \in \mathscr{T}^{\sharp}[\![P]\!].\ \Gamma(u) = Z \wedge \Gamma(u) \neq N \wedge \Gamma(v) = N$$

We say that program P respects the confidentiality property of database information, if and only if there is no information flow from private to public attributes. To verify this property, a corresponding truth assignment function $\overline{\Gamma}$ is used:

$$\overline{\Gamma}(x) = \begin{cases} T \text{ if } \Gamma(x) = H \\ F \text{ if } \Gamma(x) = L \end{cases}$$

If $\overline{\Gamma}$ does not satisfy any propositional formula in ψ of an abstract state, the analysis will report a possible information leakage.

Let us illustrate this on the running example program P in Fig. 1. According to the policy, let the database attribute corresponding to variable h_1 is private, whereas the attributes corresponding to id_1, id_2 and l_2 are public. Therefore,

$$\Gamma(\overline{h}_1) = H \text{ and } \Gamma(\overline{id}_1) = \Gamma(\overline{id}_2) = \Gamma(\overline{l}_2) = L$$

For other variables in the program, the security levels are unknown. That is,

$$\Gamma(R_1.[0]) = \Gamma(R_1.[1]) = \Gamma(\text{obj}[0]) = \Gamma(\text{obj}[1]) = \Gamma(pk) = \Gamma(h_2) = N$$

Considering the domain of positive propositional formulae, the abstract semantics yields the following formulae at program point 20 in P:

$$\overline{id}_1 \to R_1.[0]; \quad \overline{h}_1 \to R_1.[1]; \quad R_1.[0] \to \text{obj}[0];\ R_1.[1] \to \text{obj}[1];$$
$$\text{obj}[0] \to pk; \quad \text{obj}[1] \to h_2; \quad pk \to \overline{l}_2; \quad \overline{id}_2 \to \overline{l}_2; \quad h_2 \to \overline{l}_2;$$

According to the $\text{Upgrade}()$ function, the security levels of the variables with unknown security level N are upgraded as below:

$$\Gamma(R_1.[0]) = L,\ \Gamma(R_1.[1]) = H,\ \Gamma(\text{obj}[0]) = L,\ \Gamma(\text{obj}[1]) = H$$
$$\Gamma(pk) = L, \qquad \Gamma(h_2) = H$$

Finally, we apply the truth assignment function $\overline{\Gamma}$ which does not satisfy the formula $h_2 \to \overline{l}_2$, as $\overline{\Gamma}(h_2) = T$ and $\overline{\Gamma}(\overline{l}_2) = F$ and $T \to F$ is false.

Therefore, the analysis reports that the example program P is vulnerable to leakage of confidential database data.

7   Conclusions

We proposed a static analysis framework to perform information flow analysis of HQL based on the Abstract Interpretation framework. Our approach captures information leakage on "permanent" data stored in a database when a HQL program manipulates them. This may also lead to a refinement of the non-interference definition that focusses on confidentiality of the data instead of variables. We are now investigating a possible enhancement of the analysis integrating with other abstract domains. As various aggregate operations are often performed on persistent data in HQL, to consider declassification policies [30] is also our future aim. We are currently working on designing and implementing a prototype based on our proposed approach.

Acknowledgement. This work is partially supported by PRIN "Security Horizons" project and by the research grant (SB/FTP/ETA-315/2013) from the Science &Engineering Research Board (SERB), Department of Science and Technology, Government of India. We thank the anonymous reviewers for their valuable comments and suggestions.

References

1. Amtoft, T., Banerjee, A.: A logic for information flow analysis with an application to forward slicing of simple imperative programs. Sci. Comput. Program. **64**, 3–28 (2007)
2. Andrews, G.R., Reitman, R.P.: An axiomatic approach to information flow in programs. ACM Trans. Program. Lang. Syst. **2**, 56–76 (1980)
3. Bao, T., Zheng, Y., Lin, Z., Zhang, X., Xu, D.: Strict control dependence and its effect on dynamic information flow analyses. In: Proceedings of the 19th International Symposium on Software Testing and Analysis, pp. 13–24. ACM Press, Trento (2010)
4. Barbon, G., Cortesi, A., Ferrara, P., Pistoia, M., Tripp, O.: Privacy analysis of android apps: implicit flows and quantitative analysis. In: Saeed, K., Homenda, W. (eds.) CISIM 2015. LNCS, vol. 9339, pp. 3–23. Springer, New York (2015)
5. Bauer, C., King, G.: Hibernate in Action. Manning Publications Co., Greenwich (2004)
6. Bauer, C., King, G.: Java Persistence with Hibernate. Manning Publications Co., Greenwich (2006)
7. Cavadini, S.: Secure slices of insecure programs. In: Proceedings of the ACM Symposium on Information, Computer and Communications Security, pp. 112–122. ACM Press, Tokyo (2008)
8. Cortesi, A., Dovier, A., Quintarelli, E., Tanca, L.: Operational and abstract semantics of the query language G-log. Theor. Comput. Sci. **275**(1–2), 521–560 (2002)
9. Cortesi, A., Ferrara, P., Pistoia, M., Tripp, O.: Datacentric semantics for verification of privacy policy compliance by mobile applications. In: D'Souza, D., Lal, A., Larsen, K.G. (eds.) VMCAI 2015. LNCS, vol. 8931, pp. 61–79. Springer, Heidelberg (2015)
10. Cortesi, A., Halder, R.: Information-flow analysis of hibernate query language. In: Dang, T.K., Wagner, R., Neuhold, E., Takizawa, M., Küng, J., Thoai, N. (eds.) FDSE 2014. LNCS, vol. 8860, pp. 262–274. Springer, Heidelberg (2014)
11. Cousot, P., Cousot, R.: Abstract interpretation: a unified lattice model for static analysis of programs by construction or approximation of fixpoints. In: Proceedings of the POPL 1977, pp. 238–252. ACM Press, Los Angeles (1977)
12. Cousot, P., Cousot, R.: Systematic design of program analysis frameworks. In: Proceedings of the 6th ACM SIGACT-SIGPLAN Symposium on Principles of Programming Languages, pp. 269–282. ACM Press, San Antonio (1979)

13. Denning, D.E.: A lattice model of secure information flow. Commun. ACM **19**, 236–243 (1976)
14. Dimitrova, R., Finkbeiner, B., Kovács, M., Rabe, M.N., Seidl, H.: Model checking information flow in reactive systems. In: Kuncak, V., Rybalchenko, A. (eds.) VMCAI 2012. LNCS, vol. 7148, pp. 169–185. Springer, Heidelberg (2012)
15. Elliott, J., O'Brien, T., Fowler, R.: Harnessing Hibernate, 1st edn. O'Reilly, Sebastopol (2008)
16. Halder, R.: Language-based security analysis of database applications. In: Proceedings of the 3rd International Conference on Computer, Communication, Control and Information Technology (C3IT 2015), pp. 1–4. IEEE Press (2015)
17. Halder, R., Cortesi, A.: Abstract interpretation of database query languages. Comput. Lang. Syst. Struct. **38**, 123–157 (2012)
18. Halder, R., Zanioli, M., Cortesi, A.: Information leakage analysis of database query languages. In: Proceedings of the 29th Annual ACM Symposium on Applied Computing (SAC 2014), 24–28 March 2014, pp. 813–820. ACM Press, Gyeongju (2014)
19. Hammer, C.: Experiences with PDG-based IFC. In: Massacci, F., Wallach, D., Zannone, N. (eds.) ESSoS 2010. LNCS, vol. 5965, pp. 44–60. Springer, Heidelberg (2010)
20. Hammer, C., Krinke, J., Snelting, G.: Information flow control for java based on path conditions in dependence graphs. In: Proceedings of the IEEE International Symposium on Secure Software Engineering (ISSSE 2006), pp. 87–96. IEEE, Arlington (2006)
21. Hammer, C., Snelting, G.: Flow-sensitive, context-sensitive, and object-sensitive information flow control based on program dependence graphs. Int. J. Inf. Secur. **8**, 399–422 (2009)
22. Joshi, R., Leino, K.R.M.: A semantic approach to secure information flow. Sci. Comput. Program. **37**(1–3), 113–138 (2000)
23. Krinke, J.: Information flow control and taint analysis with dependence graphs. In: Proceedings of the Third International Workshop on Code Based Software Security Assessments (CoBaSSA). Technical report TUD-SERG-2007-023, Vancouver, Canada, Delft University of Technology, pp. 6–9 (2007)
24. Li, B.: Analyzing information-flow in java program based on slicing technique. SIGSOFT Softw. Eng. Notes **27**, 98–103 (2002)
25. Logozzo, F.: Class invariants as abstract interpretation of trace semantics. Comput. Lang. Syst. Struct. **35**, 100–142 (2009)
26. Mantel, H., Sudbrock, H.: Types vs. PDGs in information flow analysis. In: Albert, E. (ed.) LOPSTR 2012. LNCS, vol. 7844, pp. 106–121. Springer, Heidelberg (2013)
27. Myers, A.C.: Jflow: practical mostly-static information flow control. In: Proceedings of the 26th ACM SIGPLAN-SIGACT Symposium on Principles of Programming Languages (POPL 1999), January 20–22 1999, pp. 228–241. ACM Press, San Antonio (1999)
28. Pottier, F., Simonet, V.: Information flow inference for ML. ACM Trans. Program. Lang. Syst. **25**, 117–158 (2003)
29. Sabelfeld, A., Myers, A.C.: Language-based information-flow security. IEEE J. Sel. Areas Commun. **21**, 5–19 (2003)
30. Sabelfeld, A., Sands, D.: Declassification: dimensions and principles. J. Comput. Secur. **17**, 517–548 (2009)
31. Shroff, P., Smith, S., Thober, M.: Dynamic dependency monitoring to secure information flow. In: Proceedings of the 20th IEEE Computer Security Foundations Symposium, CSF 2007, pp. 203–217. IEEE Computer Society, Washington DC (2007). http://dx.doi.org/10.1109/CSF.2007.20

32. Smith, G.: Principles of secure information flow analysis. In: Christodorescu, M., Jha, S., Maughan, D., Song, D., Wang, C. (eds.) Malware Detection. Advances in Information Security, vol. 27, pp. 291–307. Springer, Nov Smokovec (2007)

33. Volpano, D., Irvine, C., Smith, G.: A sound type system for secure flow analysis. J. Comput. Secur. **4**, 167–187 (1996)

34. Zanioli, M., Cortesi, A.: Information leakage analysis by abstract interpretation. In: Černá, I., Gyimóthy, T., Hromkovič, J., Jefferey, K., Královič, R., Vukolić, M., Wolf, S. (eds.) SOFSEM 2011. LNCS, vol. 6543, pp. 545–557. Springer, Heidelberg (2011)

35. Zanioli, M., Ferrara, P., Cortesi, A.: Sails: static analysis of information leakage with sample. In: Proceedings of the 27th Annual ACM Symposium on Applied Computing (SAC 2012), pp. 1308–1313. ACM Press, Trento (2012)

An Adaptive Similarity Search
in Massive Datasets

Trong Nhan Phan[1(✉)], Josef Küng[1], and Tran Khanh Dang[2]

[1] Institute for Application Oriented Knowledge Processing,
Johannes Kepler University Linz, Linz, Austria
{nphan, jkueng}@faw.jku.at
[2] Faculty of Computer Science and Engineering,
HCMC University of Technology, Ho Chi Minh City, Vietnam
khanh@cse.hcmut.edu.vn

Abstract. Similarity search is an important task engaging in different fields of studies as well as in various application domains. The era of big data, however, has been posing challenges on existing information systems in general and on similarity search in particular. Aiming at large-scale data processing, we propose an adaptive similarity search in massive datasets with MapReduce. Additionally, our proposed scheme is both applicable and adaptable to popular similarity search cases such as pairwise similarity, search-by-example, range queries, and k-Nearest Neighbour queries. Moreover, we embed our collaborative refinements to effectively minimize irrelevant data objects as well as unnecessary computations. Furthermore, we experience our proposed methods with the two different document models known as shingles and terms. Last but not least, we conduct intensive empirical experiments not only to verify these methods themselves but also to compare them with a previous related work on real datasets. The results, after all, confirm the effectiveness of our proposed methods and show that they outperform the previous work in terms of query processing.

Keywords: Similarity search · Massive datasets · Scalability · Adaptivity · Collaborative filtering · Cosine · MapReduce · Hadoop

1 Introduction

The essential role of similarity search has been recognized not only in diverse fields of studies such as machine learning, data mining, clustering, and information retrieval but also in wide-ranges of applications and processes such as duplicate detection, decision support systems, search engines, and data clustering, to name a few. Its main objective is to look for other objects that are potentially similar to one another. There are different kinds of similarity search cases such as pairwise similarity, search-by-example, range queries, and k-Nearest Neighbor (k-NN) queries [13, 14].

In general, similarity search takes two main phases as follows: (1) Candidate generation phase; and (2) Verification phase. The former is to produce candidate pairs that have potential of similarity while the latter is to verify which pair is truly similar by its similarity score. The similarity search task, unfortunately, is time-consuming. For instance, doing the inceptive pairwise similarity in that all possible objects are

© Springer-Verlag Berlin Heidelberg 2016
A. Hameurlain et al. (Eds.): TLDKS XXIII, LNCS 9480, pp. 45–74, 2016.
DOI: 10.1007/978-3-662-49175-1_3

considered and computed for their self-join similarity gives an exponential complexity $O(n^2)$. Such a high cost demands either better innovations or further improvements on similarity computing.

The issue has got many attentions from both academia and industry world-wide. Some sorts of indexes or approximate but efficient approaches are proposed in order to deal with this issue [5, 6]. Nevertheless, it becomes more challenging than ever when we are in the era of big data. With the large amount of data rapidly increased, traditional processing mechanisms are in a high pressure towards their effectiveness and efficiency. Consequently, state-of-the-art tends to benefit parallel mechanism either by optimizing parallel algorithms [1] or by deploying computations on a novel parallel paradigm like MapReduce [4, 8, 12, 19, 22] to improve large-scale similarity search when dataset size never stops growing.

Being aware of the new trend and promoted by state-of-the-art, we propose an adaptive similarity search in large data collections with MapReduce. This paper is the extension of our work [14]. Our goal is to achieve an efficient large-scale processing with big data volume. Hence, our main contributions are summed up as followings:

1. We present a general similarity search scheme toward scalability and embed collaborative strategic refinements, which reduce a large amount of candidate size leading to eliminating unnecessary computing and costs, into it.
2. We effectively implement the proposed scheme with MapReduce paradigm, which supports us for large-scale data processing.
3. We show that the proposed scheme flexibly adapts itself to well-known similarity searches including pairwise similarity, search-by-example, range search, and k-Nearest Neighbor search.
4. These methods are consolidated by empirical experiments with real datasets from both DBLP [7] and Gutenberg [16] on Apache Hadoop Framework [3]. In addition, we employ the two document models known as terms and shingles to experience our proposed methods. Furthermore, these methods are evaluated and compared to the related work in [10], which shows how much beneficial they might get when processing large amount of data.

The rest of the paper is organized as follows: Sect. 2 shows related work that is pretty close to our approach. Section 3 introduces basic concepts associated with our current work. Next, we propose the general similarity search scheme in Sect. 4 and how the scheme is applicable to diverse similarity search cases in Sect. 5. Relevant experiments and analytics are then given in Sect. 6. Finally, we discuss some challenges as well as open issues towards our research work in Sect. 7 before making our final remarks in Sect. 8.

2 Related Work

Due to the importance of similarity search, many literatures have been responding the calls of its improvement against imposed new challenges whilst traditional mechanisms are not able to suitably react and gradually become out-dated. Fenz et al. show an efficient similarity search in very large string sets [11]. They propose a state set index based on a prefix index. The state set index is interpreted as a nondeterministic finite automaton. Then each character of a string is mapped to a state, and the last character defines an accepting state. Besides, they use edit distance with equal weights for operations and tune the parameters of labeling alphabet size and the index length. Nevertheless, their approach is a sequential processing while considering a set of strings instead of document objects like the way we do with MapReduce.

Xiao et al. introduce efficient similarity joins for near duplicate detection [23]. They propose an exact similarity join algorithm, together with positional filtering principle combined with both prefix and suffix filtering, to detect near-duplicates. Their approach, however, does not take parallel mode into account, which may limit the capability of processing big data volume.

Zhang et al. present a unified approximate nearest neighbor search scheme by combining data structure and hashing [24]. In their approach, they employ the prune strategy from k-means clustering tree and the fast distance computation from Hamming distance. Their goal, however, is towards only k-Nearest Neighbor queries. Moreover, these methods are done without any parallel mechanism.

Meanwhile, Alabduljalil et al. present optimized parallel algorithms for computing exactly all-pair similarity search [1]. The authors propose a hybrid indexing that combine the forward indexing and the inverted indexing on which the similarity computing is performed. In addition, they develop a partitioning method for static filtering and parallelism. The basic idea is to ensure that dissimilar objects are in different partitions. Though their methods are compatible with MapReduce paradigm, only mappers are actually involved. Besides, they introduce a circular assignment that assigns tasks computing the similarity between partitions to early remove unwanted I/O and computations. Nevertheless, they assume that the normalization from Cosine measure is already done before computing the similarity scores. We believe that the missing normalization step is really important to be effectively handled due to its extra high overheads.

Vernica et al. introduce efficient parallel set-similarity joins using MapReduce [22]. They propose a 3-stage approach for a self-join case: (1) Build a list of word frequency is in an increased order; (2) Generate a list of record-ID pairs; and (3) Output the pairs of records. Moreover, they also extend their approach for set joins and balance the workloads based on term frequencies in a round-robin manner. Nevertheless, it seems that duplicate values in each Map job are redundant, and how to calculate the similarity score is not clearly shown.

Elsayed et al. present pairwise document similarity in large collections with MapReduce [10]. Their main aim is to employ MapReduce paradigm to compute pairwise similarity by accumulating the innter product of term frequencies between a pair as follows: (1) Building a standard inverted index in that each term is associated with a list of documents to which it belongs and its corresponding term frequency; and (2) Calculating and summing all of the individual values of a pair to generate its final similarity scores. The approach looks like using Cosine measure such that the inner product of term frequency between a pair of documents is used to produce the simi-larity scores. Normalization and strategic filtering, however, are not mentioned as they are in our approach. Moreover, there is a redundancy when calculating the inner product of all pairs when given a query. In other words, the proposed method does not make the best use of the query in order to avoid such unnecessary computing as our proposed methods do.

Li et al. show batch text similarity search with MapReduce [12]. They propose a two-phase as briefly following: (1) Generate word frequency dictionary, generate vectors of all texts in the database according to the word frequency dictionary, and then generate PLT inverted file; and (2) Transform the query text into vector texts, and then calculate the prefix for each vector text. Finally, match the text which meets the requirement in PLT inverted file. The basic idea is to firstly build a word frequency dictionary. For each input, it is converted into vector texts when referenced to the dictionary. Prefixes of each vector text are then generated and stored in a PLT inverted file whose form of <word, $text_{id}$, length, threshold value>. Whenever there is a query text search, the query text is transformed into vector texts which have been later on processed for their prefixes. In the end, words in each prefix will be searched from the PLT inverted file to find the text pairs that satisfy the given similarity threshold. Unfortunately, this approach consumes lots of computations and large amounts of prefixes, which easily leads to slowing down the whole system due to the large amount of datasets.

De Francisci Morales et al. propose their approach known as scaling out all pairs similarity search with MapReduce [8]. They build inverted indexes from documents and use Cosine measure as a metric. In addition, they eliminate some terms based on a threshold and pruning techniques. Moreover, these eliminated terms are later retrieved or distributed to reduce phase to contribute to the final similarity scores. The normalization phase, however, is not mentioned.

3 Preliminaries

3.1 Concepts

A workset Ω consists of a set of N documents D_i, which is represented as $\Omega = \{D_1, D_2, D_3, ..., D_n\}$, and each document D_i composes of a set of words as $term_k$, which is shown as $D_i = \{term_1, term_2, term_3, ..., term_k\}$. In general, each document D_i has the probability to share its terms with others, and we define common terms as those contained in all the considering documents in the workset Ω. Meanwhile, each $term_k$ has its own term frequency tf_{ik}, which is described as the number of times the $term_k$ occurs in the document D_i. The inverse document frequency idf_{ik} shows how much popular a $term_k$ of a document D_i is across all the documents. In addition, there is another way to represent a document by a set of K-shingles or n-grams [17, 20]. When given a document D_i as a string of characters, K-shingles are defined as any sub-string having the length K found in the document. This concept is exploited in the field of natural language processing to represent documents and avoid the miss-match when two documents share the same number of terms but with different positions. With this model, a document D_i is alternatively represented by a set of shingles such as $D_i = \{SH_1, SH_2, ..., SH_k\}$, and the length of a document $||D_i||$ is known as the total number of shingles belonging to the document. Last but not least, the sign $[,]$ indicates a list, the sign $[[,], [,]]$ demonstrates a list of lists, the sign $[,]_{ord}$ denotes an ordered list, and $(u.v)$ gives the inner product between u and v.

In this paper, we utilize the Cosine measure, which is popular and employed by the work in [1, 4, 10, 23], to compute the similarity between a pair of documents D_i and D_j, whose formulae are defined as follows:

$$sim(D_i, D_j) = \sum_{k=1}^{t} W_{ik} * W_{jk} \qquad (1)$$

$$\text{Where } W_{ik} = \frac{tf_{ik} * \log \frac{N}{n_k}}{\sqrt{\sum_{k=1}^{t} \left[(tf_{ik})^2 * \left(\log \frac{N^2}{n_k} \right) \right]}} \qquad (2)$$

From the Eqs. (1) and (2), n_k represents the total number of documents sharing the same $term_k$, and idf_{ik} is computed as the following equation: $idf_{ik} = \log \frac{N}{n_k}$. All of the documents, however, have to be normalized before being further processed. We call W_{ik} the normalized weight of $term_k$ in the document D_i, which is done by the Eq. (2). The purpose of normalization integration is to avoid the much affection of large documents to small ones and make the similarity scores fall into the interval [0, 1], which is easily visualized to humans. Two documents are similar when the similarity score is close to 1 and vice versa. Besides, bringing the normalization into the processing makes sense in reality and not an assumption in the context of big data because of its computation costs. Last but not least, we also exploit an inverted index, which maps a $term_k$ to the document D_i to which it originally belongs, in order to speed up the processing then.

3.2 MapReduce Paradigm

MapReduce is a parallel programming paradigm which aims at many large-scale computing problems [9]. The basic idea is to divide a large problem into independent sub-problems which are then tackled in parallel by two operations known as Map and Reduce. Its mechanism is deployed on commodity machines in that one is in charge of a master node and the others are responsible for worker nodes. The master delivers m Map jobs and r Reduce jobs to workers. Those which are assigned Map jobs are called mappers whilst those which are assigned Reduce jobs are called reducers. In addition, Map jobs are specified by a Map function while Reduce jobs are defined by a Reduce function.

An overview of MapReduce paradigm is illustrated as in Fig. 1, where there are m mappers and r reducers. Each mapper has its local data in order to store the intermediate key-value pairs. Before reaching reducers, the intermediate key-value pairs are shuffled and sorted by the keys. Generally, the single flow of MapReduce can be shortly described as follows:

1. The input is partitioned in a distributed file system (e.g., Hadoop Distributed File System – HDFS) [3], which produces key-value pairs of the form *[key₁, value₁]*;
2. Mappers execute the Map function to generate intermediate key-value pairs of the form *[key₂, value₂]*;

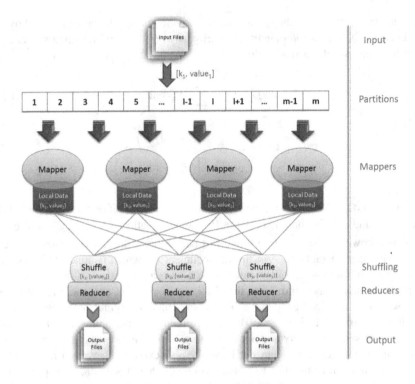

Fig. 1. The overview of MapReduce

3. The shuffling process groups these pairs into *[key₂, [value₂]]* according to the keys;
4. Reducers execute the Reduce function to output the result;
5. The result is finally written back into the distributed file system.

4   The Proposed Scheme

In this section, we propose an overview scheme that derives similarity scores between pairs of documents with MapReduce. From a general point of view and for simplicity, we firstly show the scheme as in the traditional self-join case without any query parameters in that we want to find pairwise similarity. Other specific cases following the scheme are presented in Sect. 5 of the paper. As illustrated in Fig. 2, the whole process consists of four MapReduce phases. Moreover, each phase is equipped with filtering strategies in order to eliminate dissimilar pairs and reduce overheads including storage, communication, and computing costs. The brief descriptions of these phases, along with the filtering strategies, are given as follows:

- **Phase 1 (MapReduce-1): Building the customized inverted index.** At the first MapReduce phase, sets of documents known as worksets are inputs to build the customized inverted index. The data input are split into chunks and are later on

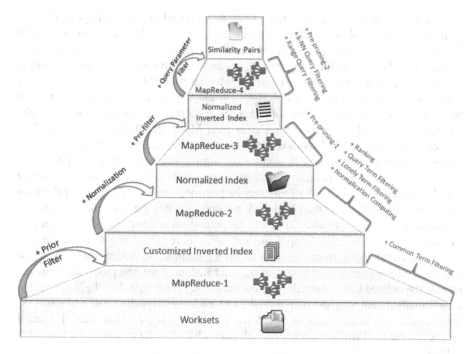

Fig. 2. The overview scheme [14]

processed in the form of key-value pairs. In addition, *Prior Filter* is applied to discard common words. The reason is that they contribute nothing to the final similarity score but give a burden to the whole process.

- **Phase 2 (MapReduce-2): Normalizing candidate pairs.** At this phase, the customized inverted index will be normalized. In parallel, *Query Term Filtering* and *Lonely Term Filtering* are applied to filter those which only exist in a single document or those which are not in the given query document, respectively. In addition, the key-value pairs are ranked in a descending manner, which is according to their values.

- **Phase 3 (MapReduce-3): Building the normalized inverted index.** These key-value pairs from MapReduce-2 are then fed to MapReduce-3 so that the normalized inverted index is generated. Besides, *Pre-pruning-1* will be done to reduce the candidate size when given a query document.

- **Phase 4 (MapReduce-4): Computing similarity pairs.** As a final phase, the normalized inverted index is employed to compute the similarity between a pair. Again, this phase filters candidate pairs according to specific query strategies like *Range Query Filtering* for range queries or *k-NN Query Filtering* for k-Nearest Neighbor (k-NN) queries before outputting similarity pairs. Moreover, it is worth noting that *Pre-pruning-2* will be utilized to reduce candidate size at the Map task of this phase before the similarity score is actually calculated. More details of each phase are given in Sect. 5 of the paper, which depends on specific similarity search cases.

The overall MapReduce operations can be summarized in Table 1. In general, let D_i be the ith document of the workset, $term_k$ be the kth word of the whole workset, tf_{ik} be the term frequency of the $term_k$ in the document D_i, idf_{ik} be the inverse document frequency of the $term_k$ in the document D_i, W_{ik} be the normalized weight of the $term_k$ in the document D_i, M_i be the total weight of all the terms in the document D_i, W_i be the largest weight of the $term_k$ in the document D_i, and $SIM(D_i, D_j)$ be the similarity score between a document pair. A special character, e.g., @, is employed to semantically separate the sub-values in the values of a pair. More specifically, the intermediate key-value pairs after Map-1 method are of the form $[term_k, D_i]$, which are then fed to Reduce-1 method so that we can acquire the normalized inverted index of the form $[term_k, [D_i@tf_{ik}@idf_{ik}]]$. In order to normalize the weight of the $term_k$ in the document D_i, Map-2 method is in charge of emitting its intermediate key-value pairs of the form $[D_i, term_k@tf_{ik}@idf_{ik}]$ and then Reduce-2 method executes the normalization process according to the Eqs. (1) and (2) before outputting an ordered list of the form $[D_i, [term_k@W_{ik}]]_{ord}$. After that, Map-3 method takes its responsibility to build the normalized inverted index from the ordered list by emitting its intermediate key-value pairs of the form $[term_k, D_i@M_i@W_i@W_{ik}]$ and Reduce-3 method processes them and outputs the ordered key-value pairs of the form $[term_k, [D_i@M_i@W_i@W_{ik}]]_{ord}$. Finally, Map-4 method computes the partial product of each corresponding pair and emits the intermediate key-value pairs of the form $[D_{ij}, (W_{ik}. W_{jk})]$. After that, Reduce-4 aggregates the final similarity score of each pair, which has the output of the form $[D_{ij}, SIM(D_i, D_j)]$.

Table 1. The overall MapReduce operations [14]

Task	Input	Output
MAP-1	$[worksets]$	$[term_k, D_i]$
REDUCE-1	$[term_k, D_i]$	$[term_k, [D_i@tf_{ik}@idf_{ik}]]$
MAP-2	$[term_k, [D_i@tf_{ik}@idf_{ik}]]$	$[D_i, term_k@tf_{ik}@idf_{ik}]$
REDUCE-2	$[D_i, term_k@tf_{ik}@idf_{ik}]$	$[D_i, term_k@W_{ik}]_{ord}$
MAP-3	$[D_i, term_k@W_{ik}]_{ord}$	$[term_k, D_i@M_i@W_i@W_{ik}]$
REDUCE-3	$[term_k, D_i@M_i@W_i@W_{ik}]$	$[term_k, [D_i@M_i@W_i@W_{ik}]_{ord}]$
MAP-4	$[term_k, [D_i@M_i@W_i@W_{ik}]_{ord}]$	$[D_{ij}, (W_{ik} \cdot W_{jk})]$
REDUCE-4	$[D_{ij}, (W_{ik} \cdot W_{jk})]$	$[D_{ij}, SIM(D_i, D_j)]$

5   Similarity Search Cases

The proposed scheme is applicable not only to popular similarity searches like pairwise similarity and search-by-example but also to those with query strategies such as range search and k-NN search. In each sub section below, we show in detail how it gets insight on the specific similarity searches.

5.1   Pairwise Similarity

Pairwise similarity search is the case in that we want to find out all possible similar pairs. In other words, one is bound to every other to give their similarity. Following the scheme, worksets are initially passed to mappers at Map-1 method, which produces intermediate key-value pairs of the form $[term_k, D_i]$. They are then retrieved by reducers at Reducer-1 method to output the key-value pairs of the form $[term_k, [D_i@tf_{ik}@idf_{ik}]]$, where tf_{ik} and idf_{ik} are derived. At this step, common words which have idf_{ik} equal to 0 are discarded by the *Prior Filter*. For example, assuming that there are three documents named D_1, D_2, and D_3, and each document contains its corresponding words as the input illustrated in Fig. 3. After Map-1 method, we have a list of intermediate key-value pairs [[A, D_1], [B, D_1], [B, D_1], [C, D_1], [A, D_1], [E, D_1], [C, D_2], [A, D_2], [D, D_3], [B, D_3], [A, D_3], [E, D_3]]. The list is then accessed by reducers at Reduce-1 method. The common word A is ignored by the *Common Term Filtering* while the lonely word D is marked as *Terms Not Proceeded-{TNP}*. The reason why the lonely word D is not discarded right away but marked as a special sign at this phase is that it should be kept joining the normalization step later on even though it does not contribute to any similarity scores in the end. Therefore, we have the output list of the form of key-value pairs as follows [[B, [D_1@2@0.176, D_3@1@0.176]], [C, [D_1@1@0.176, D_2@1@0.176]], [{TNP}, D_3@1@0.477]], [E, [D_1@1@0.176, D_3@1@0.176]]].

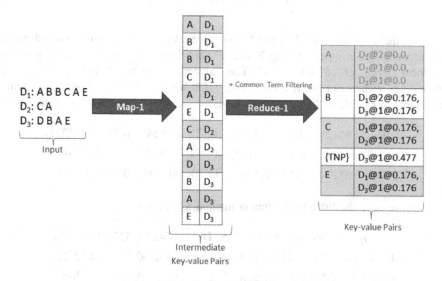

Fig. 3. MapReduce-1 operation [14]

Next, the key-value pairs from the first MapReduce are normalized at the second MapReduce. The intermediate key-value pairs after Map-2 method have the form of $[D_i, term_k@tf_{ik}@idf_{ik}]$. The Reduce-2 method normalizes these pairs into an ordered list of the form $[D_i, [term_k@W_{ik}]]_{ord}$. The values are sorted by their sizes and then by their W_{ik}. Figure 4 shows the ongoing example at the second MapReduce. The mappers at Map-2 method output the intermediate key-value pairs as the list [[D_1, B@2@0.176], [D_3, B@1@0.176], [D_1, C@1@0.176], [D_2, C@1@0.176], [D_3, {TNP}@1@0.477], [D_1, E@1@0.176], [D_3, E@1@0.176]]. These pairs are later normalized by the reducers at Reduce-2 method which gives us the normalized and ordered output list as following [[D_1, [B@0.8165, C@0.4082, E@0.4082]], [D_3, [B@0.3271, E@0.3271]], [D_2, [C@0.1760]]]. It is worth noting that the lonely term *{TNP}* is filtered by *Lonely Term Filtering* at Reduce-2 method.

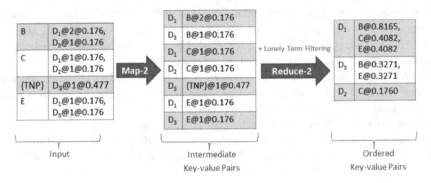

Fig. 4. MapReduce-2 operation [14]

After the normalization, the third MapReduce takes the normalized inverted index into account. The mappers at Map-3 method emit the intermediate key-value pairs of the form *[term_k, D_i@M_i@W_i@W_{ik}]*. The reducers at Reduce-3 method output the ordered key-value pairs of the form *[term_k, [D_i@M_i@W_i@W_{ik}]]_ord*. Figure 5 presents the ongoing example at this phase. We have the list after Map-3 method as follows:

[[B, D_3@0.6542@0.3271@0.3271], [E, D_3@0.6542@0.3271@0.3271],
 [B, D_1@1.6329@0.8165@0.8165], [C, D_1@1.6329@0.8165@0.4082],
 [E, D_1@1.6329@0.8165@0.4082], [C, D_2@0.1760@0.1760@0.1760]]

And we have the list after Reduce-3 method as follows:

[[B, [D_1@1.6329@0.8165@0.8165, D_3@0.6542@0.3271@0.3271]],
 [E, [D_1@1.6329@0.8165@0.4082, D_3@0.6542@0.3271@0.3271]],
 [C, D1@1.6329@0.8165@0.4082, D_2@0.1760@0.1760@0.1760]]].

Finally, the fourth MapReduce computes the partial product of each corresponding term of a pair, which has the form *[D_{ij}, (W_{ik}. W_{jk})]*, at Map-4 method and leads to the final similarity score of each pair, which has the form *[D_{ij}, SIM(D_i, D_j)]* after Reduce-4 method. The running example is closed at this phase from Fig. 6. The intermediate key-value pairs [[D_{13}, 0.2881], [D_{12}, 0.0718], [D_{13}, 0.1440]] after Map-4 method are

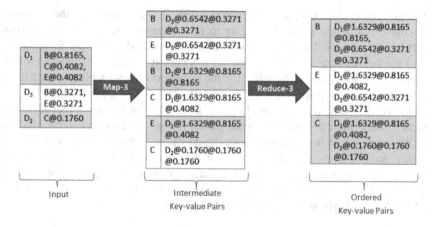

Fig. 5. MapReduce-3 operation [14]

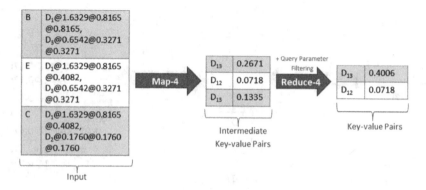

Fig. 6. MapReduce-4 operation [14]

aggregated to the final similarity scores $[[D_{13}, 0.4321], [D_{12}, 0.0718]]$ at Reduce-4 method. Last but not least, *Query Parameter Filtering* is optionally applied to obtain closer results when query parameters are given.

5.2 Search-by-Example

Search-by-example is a well-known similarity search case when given a pivot object as an example for the search. The goal is to find the most similar objects according to the pivot. Once it is the case, not only are lonely words in the pivot discarded but also those which do not exist in the pivot are ignored by *Lonely Term Filtering* and *Query Term Filtering* at Reduce-2 method. The reason is that they do not contribute to the similarity between a pair but make the process bulky. Doing so significantly contributes to the reduction of overheads such as storage, communication, and computing costs through the whole process of MapReduce jobs.

Let us come to the example as illustrated in Fig. 7, and at this time, the document D_3 is considered as the pivot. According to the proposed scheme, the intermediate key-value pairs emitted from the mappers at Map-1 method are of the form *[term$_k$, D$_i$]* and the key-value pairs output from the reducers at Reduce-1 method are of the form *[term$_k$, [D$_i$@tf$_{ik}$@idf$_{ik}$]]*. Specifically, the mappers at Map-1 method emit a list of intermediate key-value pairs [[A, D_1], [B, D_1], [B, D_1], [C, D_1], [A, D_1], [E, D_1], [C, D_2], [A, D_2], [D, D_3], [B, D_3], [A, D_3], [E, D_3]]. The list is later retrieved by the reducers to build the customized inverted index. Again, the *Common Term Filtering* filters the word A that is common among the documents whereas the lonely word D belonging to D_3 is marked as *Terms Not Proceeded-{TNP}*. Consequently, the key-value pairs list from the reducers at Reduce-1 method is output as follows [[B, [D_1@2@0.176, D_3@1@0.176]], [C, [D_1@1@0.176, D_2@1@0.176]], [{TNP}, D_3@1@0.477]], [E, [D_1@1@0.176, D_3@1@0.176]]].

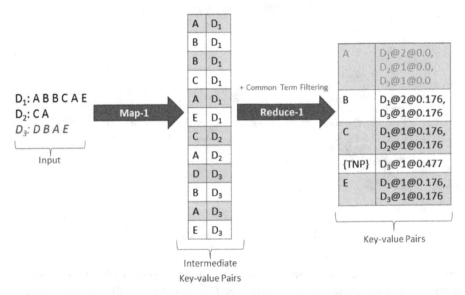

Fig. 7. MapReduce-1 operation when given the pivot [14]

Then we come to the normalization phase at the second MapReduce as illustrated in Fig. 8. At this phase, the intermediate key-value pairs emitted from Map-2 method are of the form *[D$_i$, term$_k$@tf$_{ik}$@idf$_{ik}$]* before being normalized at Reduce-2 method into an ordered list of the form *[D$_i$, [term$_k$@W$_{ik}$]]$_{ord}$*. More concretely, the mappers at Map-2 method emit the intermediate key-value pairs as the list [[D_1, B@2@0.176], [D_3, B@1@0.176], [D_1, C@1@0.176], [D_2, C@1@0.176], [D_3, {TNP}@1@0.477], [D_1, E@1@0.176], [D_3, E@1@0.176]]. After that, these pairs are normalized by the reducers at Reduce-2 method which gives us the normalized and ordered output list [[D_1, [B@0.8165, E@0.4082]], [D_3, [B@0.3271, E@0.3271]]]. It is worth noting that the lonely term *{TNP}* is filtered by *Lonely Term Filtering* at Reduce-2 method. Besides, the *Query Term Filtering* is in active due to the fact that we are in the case of

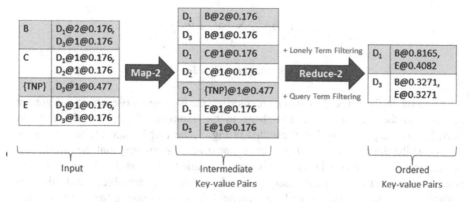

Fig. 8. MapReduce-2 operation when given the pivot [14]

search-by-example. Thus, the word C in D_1 and the word C in D_2 which are not included in the pivot D_3 are discarded in advance as shown in Fig. 8.

The other two MapReduce operations (i.e., MapReduce-3 and MapReduce-4) conform to the proposed scheme as the examples in Figs. 5 and 6. Furthermore, search-by-example can be leveraged by query strategies presented in Sect. 5.3, which shows how soon candidate pairs are filtered to reduce the candidate size and make them themselves fit the query.

5.3   Query Strategies

Most similarity searches are also accompanied with search query strategies such as range search or k-NN search. The range search adds the similarity threshold ε so that those pairs whose similarity is greater or equal to the threshold should be returned as the final result. Meanwhile, the k-NN search looks for the k most similar objects from the candidate sets. As a consequence, the parameters ε and k are utilized to filter objects so that the final result, on the one hand, is as close as users' needs and the search process, on the other hand, is significantly improved. In order to exploit them for the proposed scheme, both *Pre-pruning-1*, for the case a query document is given, and *Pre-pruning-2*, for other cases, are attached but not mutually exclusive.

In the case of pairwise similarity, we do not actually want to find all-pair similarity due to the fact that it is rarely used in a specific range of applications whereas its entire result is not completely utilized. Moreover, such a big process consumes much time and resources, which is not really suitable for most application scenarios, especially for real-time intensive ones. Thus, the threshold ε is provided to filter necessary pairs from the total candidates to meet certain needs. *Pre-pruning-2* at Map-4 method catches this line of thought. It employs the two below inequalities with the latter adopted in [1] to do its task as candidate filtering:

$$sim(D_i, D_j) = \sum_{k=1}^{t} W_{ik} * W_{jk} \geq \varepsilon \tag{3}$$

$$sim(D_i, D_j) \leq \min(M_i * W_j, M_j * W_i) = \sigma \tag{4}$$

From the inequalities (3) and (4), the filtering rule is to find those whose σ is greater or equal to the threshold ε. Let us back to the example of pairwise similarity in Sect. 5.1. At Map-4 method as illustrated in Fig. 9, the pair D_1 and D_3 has their σ as 0.5341 whilst the pair D_1 and D_2 has their σ as 0.1437. Assuming that the threshold ε has the value 0.4, the pair D_1 and D_2 is early discarded. Meanwhile, *Pre-pruning-1* is able to sooner get rid of unnecessary pairs when given a query object, and this supporting process takes place at Reduce-3 method. It is worth noting that the key-value pairs at this phase have the form *[term$_k$, D_i@M_i@W_i@W_{ik}]*, so the above filtering rule can be shortly derived. From the instance of search-by-example in Sect. 5.2, the *Pre-pruning-1* method indicated in Fig. 10 estimates candidate pairs whether σ is greater or equal to ε. The value of σ is computed as 0.4006, which is the minimum between 0.4006 and 0.5342. Assuming the threshold ε has the value 0.4, the pair D_1 and D_3 is, therefore, further processed to get their final similarity.

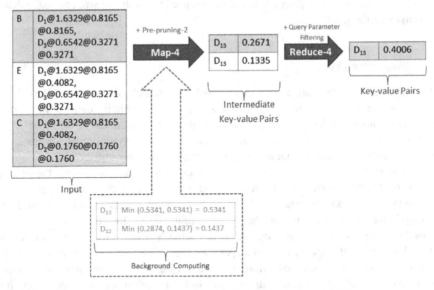

Fig. 9. MapReduce-4 operation with Pre-pruning-2 [14]

On the other hand, k-NN query is also attached together with a query object. *Pre-pruning-1* takes the k parameter into account to filter objects before their similarity is computed. In other words, each mapper at Map-3 method approximately emits top-k key-value pairs whose size is according to the total number of running mappers as the Eq. (5) below:

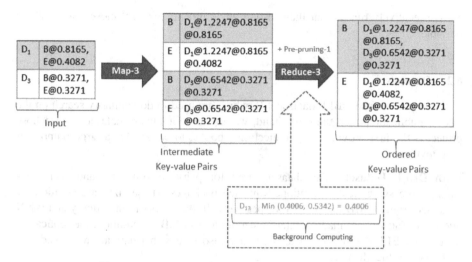

Fig. 10. MapReduce-3 operation with Pre-pruning-1 [14]

$$\underset{\substack{\text{for each mapper}}}{\text{top} - \text{k pairs}} = \max_{k \in N}\left(\frac{k}{\sum Mappers}, 1\right) \tag{5}$$

It is totally possible because the key-value pair input of Map-3 method has been ordered by its size and normalized weights from the second MapReduce operation. Moreover, the probability a pair is the most similar is high when each combined object has its largest size and normalized weights. As a consequence, the Eq. (5) helps reduce both unnecessary computing and the candidate size.

6   Experiments

6.1   Environment Settings

In order to do our experiments with MapReduce, we employ the stable version 1.2.1 of Hadoop [3]. The Hadoop framework is deployed in the cluster of commodity machines called Alex, which has 48 nodes and 8 CPU cores with either 96 or 48 GB RAM for each node [2]. In general, we leave Hadoop configurations in default mode as much as possible, for we want to keep the most initial settings which a commodity machine may get even though some parameters could be tuned or optimized to fit the Alex cluster. The configured capacity is set to 5 GB per node, so the 48-node cluster totally has 240 GB. The number of reducers for a reduce operation is set to 168. The possible heap size of the cluster is about 629 MB, and each HDFS file has 64 MB Block Size. It is worth noting that Alex has suffered the overhead of other coordinating parallel tasks, i.e., these nodes are not exclusively for the experiments. Last but not least, each benchmark has its fresh running. In other words, data from the old benchmark are removed before the new benchmark starts. All the experiments for one type of query are consecutively run so that their testing environments are kept closely as much as possible.

6.2 Datasets

In this paper, we use DBLP datasets [7], which are used to do similarity search on the title of publications. On the other hand, we also use Gutenberg datasets [16], whose project is the first provider of free electronic books, to experience a large number of long text files.

With DBLP Datasets. The datasets used for pairwise similarity and search-by-example are synthetically partitioned into ten packages whose sizes are additionally increased from 50 MB to 500 MB, respectively. In the cases of range query and k-NN query, the datasets are made greater in size up to 700 MB. In addition, the replication factor for DBLP datasets is set to 47, which also means that data are replicated into each node in the cluster.

With Gutenberg Datasets. The datasets for pairwise similarity and search-by-example are divided into five packages separately including 1000 files, 1500 files, 2000 files, 2500 files, and 3000 files. These files which are randomly selected from the Gutenberg repository have their sizes ranging from 15 KB to 100 KB. Unlike DBLP datasets, the replication factor used for Gutenberg datasets is preserved as 3 as its default block replication.

6.3 Experiment Measurement

For our experiments, we step-by-step evaluate our proposed methods and the related work as following:

- *The naïve self-join:* indicates the self-join approach without any filtering.
- *The filtering self-join:* implies the self-join approach with filtering.
- *Search-by-example:* mentions the case when given an object as an example for the search.
- *Range-query case:* shows the case of similarity search when given a similarity threshold ε.
- *k-NN query case:* denotes the case of searching for k most similar objects from the candidate sets.
- *Pivot case:* refers to the case doing pairwise similarity when given a query.
- *The work in 2008* [10]: builds the standard inverted index and term frequencies and then employ them to compute similarity between a pair by their inner product. This work only consumes two MapReduce phases due to the fact that normalization phase is omitted.

Moreover, we experience the two document models known as terms model and shingles model in Sect. 3.1. The former represents a document as a set of terms whilst the latter represents a document as a set of shingles. Furthermore, we are interested in both the performance and the data volume of the proposed methods and the related method, which is described as follows:

Performance Measurement. We measure the execution time of MapReduce jobs known as the total processing time. The measuring time is bound since the time MapReduce jobs start running to the time they finish writing the result to the distributed file system. Moreover, we also separately consider the measuring time for each MapReduce job. And from this point of view, the better performance actually costs less processing time.

Data Volume Measurement. We observe how much data are produced throughout MapReduce jobs and are then written into the distributed file system. The goal is to find out how much the data volumes output and written to the distributed file system give influences to the performance in overall.

6.4   Empirical Evaluations with DBLP Datasets

In this section, we perform some performance measurements for examining our methods. First, Fig. 11 shows Pairwise similarity case with DBLP datasets among the naïve self-join, the filtering self-join, and the work in 2008 [10] and search-by-example. Apart from the work in 2008, the other approaches are based on our proposed scheme in Sect. 4. Besides, we also compare the search-by-example case with the pairwise similarity case. The dataset size is increased turn by turn from 50 MB to 500 MB. From Fig. 11a, the result shows that our proposed methods outperform the work in 2008 in terms of query processing time. More concretely on the average, the naïve self-join is 68.38 % faster than the work in 2008, the filtering self-join is 69.41 % faster than the work in 2008, and the search-by-example is 73.03 % faster than the work in 2008. The main reason is that the work in 2008 finds the term frequency right away at mappers instead of reducers whose main goal is to perform reduced computations. In other words, the functionality of mappers is mistakenly used from the beginning. Moreover, the work in 2008 computes all possible candidates without filtering whilst our approach does. On the other hand, there is no big difference among the naïve approach, the filtering self-join, and search-by-example while the dataset size is still small, or to say, under a specific threshold. The reason is due to the operation cost of the whole system. Once the dataset size is significantly increased, a big gap among them emerges. On the average, the naïve self-join consumes 3.5 % more CPU time than the filtering self-join and 15.1 % more CPU time than search-by-example.

In terms of data volumes, Fig. 11b shows the correlation of data quantity among the approaches throughout MapReduce operations with DBLP datasets. The work in 2008 has fewer amounts of data output in the end. More specifically, the work in 2008 produces 75.21 % less data than the naïve self-join, 72.61 % less data than the filtering self-join, and 17.70 % less data than search-by-example, respectively on the average. The reason is that the proposed scheme, on the one hand, needs to normalize inputs before computing the similarity whilst no filtering is accompanied. On the other hand, it is worth noticing that the work in 2008 computes the similarity score between two documents by summing the inner products of the term frequencies, which are not

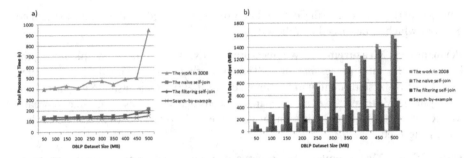

Fig. 11. Similarity-computing performance with DBLP datasets among the naïve self-join, the filtering self-join, the work in 2008 and search-by-example; (a) the total processing time; and (b) the saved data volume [14] (Color figure online)

normalized yet. Normalization is essential because weight terms should be high if they are frequent in relevant documents but infrequent in the collection as a whole. If normalization is taken into account, the work in 2008 suffers more computations and data volumes. Nevertheless, we implement it as the original version, i.e., without normalization. Furthermore, the result indicates how much important the refinements are applied in order for the filtering self-join to save 8.67 % data quantity and for search-by-example to save 69.78 % data quantity, on the average, when compared to the naïve self-join. Last but not least, the amount of data output from MapReduce-2 operation to MapReduce-4 operation, when filtering is applied, just gets 0.04 % data proportion on the average compared to the whole data output in the case of search-by-example itself. As a consequence, search-by-example has less data than the naïve self-join. In summary, the data output volume without filtering is nearly double in comparison with the data input size due to normalization. In addition, MapReduce mechanism always writes down intermediate outputs into HDFS, whose disk access costs are too expensive. Filtering strategies are, therefore, essential to reduce the candidate size and related computing costs as well.

On the other side, we conduct experiments with query strategies when the DBLP dataset size is step-by-step increasing from 300 MB to 700 MB, which are shown in Fig. 12. The data values from Fig. 12a indicate that there is no big difference in terms of query processing among range queries where the similarity thresholds are set to 90 %, 70 %, and 50 %. Likewise, the values from Fig. 12b point out the same evaluation for k-NN queries where the values of parameter k are set to 100, 300, and 500, respectively. Moreover, the two kinds of query strategies mostly have the same performance. In other words, either the parameter ε for range queries or the parameter k for k-NN queries does not give a big gap between them. Last but not least, the two kinds of query strategies perform from 2.67 % to 4 % faster than search-by-example without pre-pruning.

6.5   Empirical Evaluations with Gutenberg Datasets

When working with Gutenberg datasets for pairwise similarity, both the naïve self-join and the work in 2008 fail right away with 3000 Gutenberg files in the second Reduce

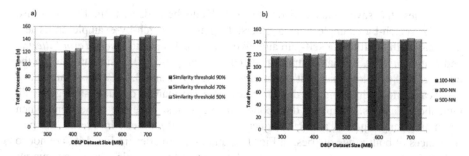

Fig. 12. Query strategies with DBLP datasets; (a) range query case; and (b) k-NN query case [14] (Color figure online)

operations because of out of memory at reducers. This means that the reducers work with massive key-value pairs that get over their memory capacity. Nevertheless, the filtering self-join, pivot case (i.e., the case does pairwise similarity when given a query), and search-by-example get rid of that problem due to the fact that they are equipped with filtering strategies that help reduce candidate size. Figure 13 illustrates, therefore, the similarity-computing performance among the filtering self-join, pivot case, and search-by-example in Gutenberg datasets. In general, the performances among them, as seen in Fig. 13a, are not much different when the number of files increases from 1000 files to 2000 files. The performance among them has, however, a gap when the number of files increases from 2000 files to 3000 files. This implies that both pivot case and search-by-example perform better than the filtering self-join with the average rates as 7.06 % and 5.74 %, respectively. The important key basically comes from the fact that both pivot case and search-by-example deal with candidates more efficiently than the filtering self-join does. Other than *Lonely Term Filtering*, both pivot case and search-by-example take the advantage of *Query Term Filtering* when given a pivot object. In other words, both of them avoid the outbreak case in the filtering self-join, which has to compute similarity scores between one document and every other in the corpus.

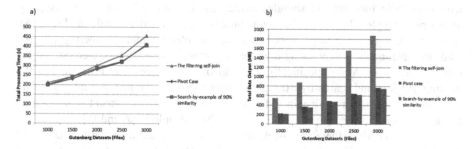

Fig. 13. Similarity-computing performance with Gutenberg datasets between the filtering self-join and search-by-example; (a) the total processing time; and (b) the saved data volume (Color figure online)

Besides, the saved data experiments with Gutenberg datasets in Fig. 13b also promote search-by-example among others. In general, search-by-example emits less data than both the filtering self-join and pivot case do. Thanks to *Query Term Filtering* and *Pre-pruning-2*, the data output of search-by-example of 90 % similarity is, on the average, 59.84 % less than that of the filtering self-join and 3.13 % less than that of pivot case. Meanwhile, Fig. 14 demonstrates the performances of query strategies with Gutenberg datasets. From the data collected, we almost have the same trend when examining range queries and k-NN queries with DBLP datasets. In overall, the performances of both range queries, in Fig. 14a, and k-NN queries, in Fig. 14b, are not so different. On the average when compared to search-by-example, the range queries perform 1.24 % to 2.67 % faster when the similarity threshold changes from 90 %, 70 %, and 50 % whilst the k-NN queries have the speed-up rates from 3.18 % to 3.85 % when the values of parameter k are set to 100, 300, and 500, respectively.

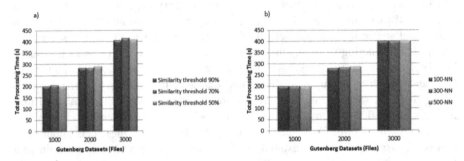

Fig. 14. Query strategies with Gutenberg datasets; (a) range query case; and (b) k-NN query case (Color figure online)

6.6 Empirical Evaluations Between Terms and Shingles

In these experiments, we want to evaluate our methods with shingles instead of terms. In other words, each document in the Gutenberg datasets is respectively represented as a set of terms and a set of shingles. As the data outbreak of pairwise similarity in the work 2008 and the naïve self-join, Fig. 15 shows the similarity-computing performance with Gutenberg datasets and shingles among the filtering self-join, pivot case, and search-by-example. In terms of total processing time illustrated in Fig. 15a, search-by-example tends to perform better than the others while the filtering self-join tends to consume more processing time than the others. Nevertheless, there are no big gaps among them. More specifically, the gap of total processing time between the filtering self-join and search-by-example is around 0.26 %, the gap of total processing time between the filtering self-join and pivot case is around 0.86 %, and the gap of total processing time between pivot case and search-by-example is around 0.15 %.

On the other hand, there are visible differences among these similarity searches in the view of the saved data volume as seen in Fig. 15b. Like what we have got when doing this kind of experiments with terms, the filtering strategies really work. In general, search-by-example keeps emitting the less total data output whilst the filtering

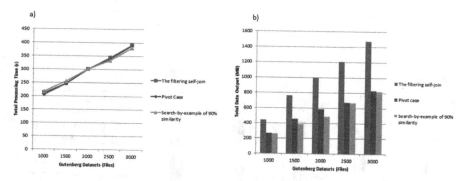

Fig. 15. Similarity-computing performance with Gutenberg datasets and shingles among the filtering self-join, pivot case, and search-by-example; (a) the total processing time; and (b) the saved data volume (Color figure online)

self-join does the most. Besides, the total data output in pivot case is a bit more in that of search-by-example but much less than that of the filtering self-join. More specifically, the percentage difference of total data output between the filtering self-join and search-by-example is around 46.07 %, the percentage difference of total data output between the filtering self-join and pivot case is around 41.77 %, and the percentage difference of total data output between pivot case and search-by-example is around 7.26 %. The reason behind that makes the big gap between the filtering self-join and the others is mostly from the *Query Term Filtering*. In this case, it filters shingles by the query shingles.

To compare the similarity-computing performance when the documents are represented as terms and shingles, we separately compare our methods into pairs. For the performance comparison, we turn-by-turn show the total processing time of not only the whole MapReduce operation, which is known as Total MR, but also the four MapReduce sub-operations, which are called MR-1, MR-2, MR-3, and MR-4, respectively. From now on, the left axis presents for the four sub-operations whereas the right axis presents for the whole operations. Firstly, we compare the filtering self-join with terms and shingles. Figure 16 demonstrates the performance of the filtering self-join between them. Generally, the total MR with shingles performs better than that with terms. On the one hand, the most time-consuming MapReduce operation among one another falls into MR-1, which has to process large amounts of data and compute term frequency as well as the inverse document frequency at the same time. On the other hand, MR-4 also takes time to produce candidate pairs and the final similarity scores. The others, MR-2 and MR-3, consume less time in comparison with MR-1 and MR-4. More specifically in the comparison between terms and shingles, the maximum difference between MR-1 with terms and MR-1 with shingles is about 10.14 %, the maximum difference between MR-2 with terms and MR-2 with shingles is about 11.43 %, the maximum difference between MR-3 with terms and MR-3 with shingles is about 7.5 %, the maximum difference between MR-4 with terms and MR-4 with shingles is about 44.32 %, and the maximum difference between Total MR with terms and Total MR with shingles is about 14.25 %.

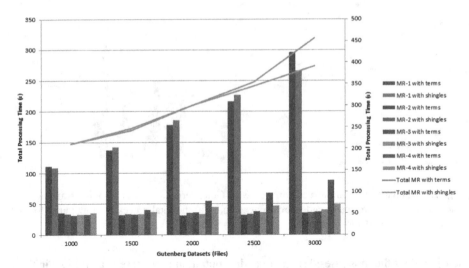

Fig. 16. The performance of the filtering self-join with terms and shingles (Color figure online)

In terms of data output, the total data output with shingles is generally much less than that with terms as showed in Fig. 17. Although MR-3 operation takes little time to complete, it emits the most data compared to the others. On the contrary, MR-4 takes more time than MR-3 but produces the least data output. More specifically in the comparison between terms and shingles, the maximum difference between MR-1 with terms and MR-1 with shingles is about 7.66 %, the maximum difference between MR-2 with terms and MR-2 with shingles is about 19.82 %, the maximum difference between MR-3 with terms and MR-3 with shingles is about 37.37 %, the maximum difference between MR-4 with terms and MR-4 with shingles is about 27.85 %, and the maximum difference between Total MR with terms and Total MR with shingles is about 22.67 %.

Secondly, we compare pivot case with terms and shingles. Figure 18 demonstrates the performance of pivot case between them. In general, the total MR with shingles performs better than that with terms only in the data package of 3000 files. In the other data packages, the total MR with terms performs better than that with shingles. As usual, the most time-consuming MapReduce operation falls into MR-1. On the other hand, the others take not much time to complete their jobs. In particular, the maximum difference between MR-1 with terms and MR-1 with shingles is about 14.05 %, the maximum difference between MR-2 with terms and MR-2 with shingles is about 19.15 %, the maximum difference between MR-3 with terms and MR-3 with shingles is about 9.09 %, the maximum difference between MR-4 with terms and MR-4 with shingles is about 29.79 %, and the maximum difference between Total MR with terms and Total MR with shingles is about 6.62 %.

In the point of view of data output, the total data output with shingles is generally more than that with terms as showed in Fig. 19. In this case, MR-1 is the one which emits the most data output while MR-4 is the one which produces the least. By observing, the total data output from MR-4 is much less than that of MR-1, MR-2, and MR-3, even with either terms or shingles. Specifically in the comparison between terms

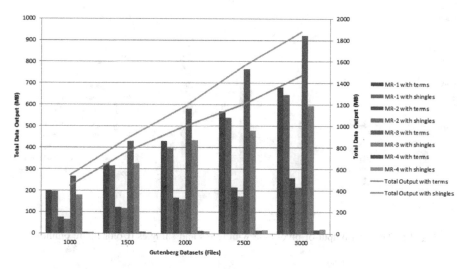

Fig. 17. The data output of the filtering self-join with terms and shingles (Color figure online)

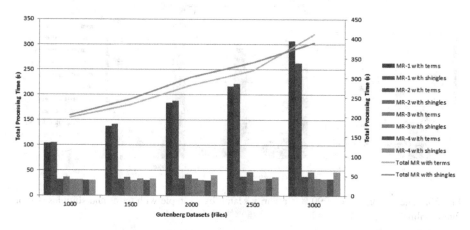

Fig. 18. The performance of pivot case with terms and shingles (Color figure online)

and shingles, the maximum difference between MR-1 with terms and MR-1 with shingles is about 7.66 %, the maximum difference between MR-2 with terms and MR-2 with shingles is about 76.86 %, the maximum difference between MR-3 with terms and MR-3 with shingles is about 65.09 %, the maximum difference between MR-4 with terms and MR-4 with shingles is about 40.04 %, and the maximum difference between Total MR with terms and Total MR with shingles is about 19.20 %.

Thirdly, we compare search-by-example with terms and shingles when the similarity threshold is set to 90 %. Figure 20 illustrates the performance of 90 %-similarity search-by-example between them. Similarly with pivot case, the total MR with shingles performs better than that with terms only in the data package of 3000 files. In the other data packages, the total MR with terms performs better than that with shingles. One

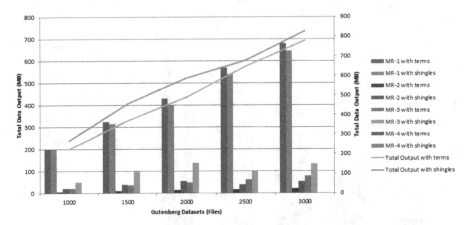

Fig. 19. The data output of pivot case with terms and shingles (Color figure online)

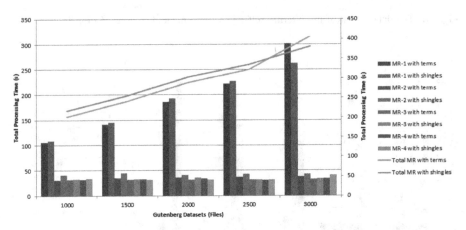

Fig. 20. The performance of 90 %-similarity search-by-example with terms and shingles (Color figure online)

again, the most time-consuming MapReduce operation falls into MR-1. On the other side, the others take not much time to complete their jobs. What is more, the maximum difference between MR-1 with terms and MR-1 with shingles is about 12.62 %, the maximum difference between MR-2 with terms and MR-2 with shingles is about 24.39 %, the maximum difference between MR-3 with terms and MR-3 with shingles is about 11.11 %, the maximum difference between MR-4 with terms and MR-4 with shingles is about 17.07 %, and the maximum difference between Total MR with terms and Total MR with shingles is about 7.37 %.

In the meantime, the total data output with shingles is generally more than that with terms as indicated in Fig. 21. And at this time, MR-1 is the one which emits the most data output while MR-4 produces the least. Nevertheless, the total data output from MR-4 is much less than that of MR-1, MR-2, and MR-3, even with either terms or

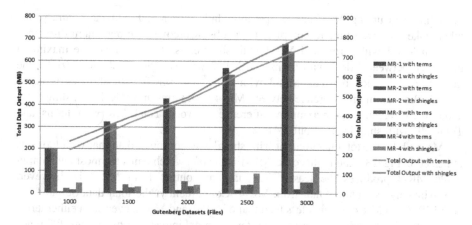

Fig. 21. The data output of 90 %-similarity search-by-example with terms and shingles (Color figure online)

shingles. In the comparison between terms and shingles, the maximum difference between MR-1 with terms and MR-1 with shingles is about 7.66 %, the maximum difference between MR-2 with terms and MR-2 with shingles is about 76.88 %, the maximum difference between MR-3 with terms and MR-3 with shingles is about 71.08 %, the maximum difference between MR-4 with terms and MR-4 with shingles is about 73.90 %, and the maximum difference between Total MR with terms and Total MR with shingles is about 17.27 %.

Finally, we compare k-NN queries with terms and shingles when the parameter k is set to 500. Figure 22 presents the performance of 500-NN queries between them. In these experiments, we observe that the total MR with shingles slightly performs better than that with terms only in the data package of 3000 files. In the other data packages, the total MR with terms performs pretty better than that with shingles. Normally, the

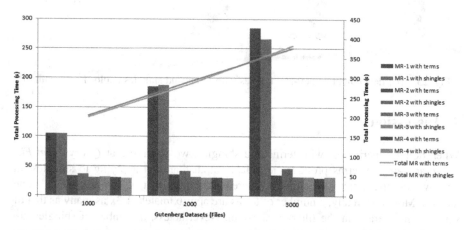

Fig. 22. The performance of 500-NN queries with terms and shingles (Color figure online)

most time-consuming MapReduce operation falls into MR-1. On the contrary, the others take not much time to complete their jobs. Moreover, the maximum difference between MR-1 with terms and MR-1 with shingles is about 6.67 %, the maximum difference between MR-2 with terms and MR-2 with shingles is about 23.91 %, the maximum difference between MR-3 with terms and MR-3 with shingles is about 3.13 %, the maximum difference between MR-4 with terms and MR-4 with shingles is about 6.25 %, and the maximum difference between Total MR with terms and Total MR with shingles is about 2.41 %.

Meanwhile, the total data output with shingles is not much than that with terms as indicated in Fig. 23. And in this case, MR-1 is the one which emits the most data output while MR-4 produces the least. The total data output from MR-3 is, however, approximately as small as that from MR-4. Consequently, the total data output from both MR-3 and MR-4 is much less than that of MR-1 and MR-2, even with either terms or shingles. In the comparison between terms and shingles, the maximum difference between MR-1 with terms and MR-1 with shingles is about 7.65 %, the maximum difference between MR-2 with terms and MR-2 with shingles is about 76.86 %, the maximum difference between MR-3 with terms and MR-3 with shingles is about 30.54 %, the maximum difference between MR-4 with terms and MR-4 with shingles is about 2.77 %, and the maximum difference between Total MR with terms and Total MR with shingles is about 5.69 %.

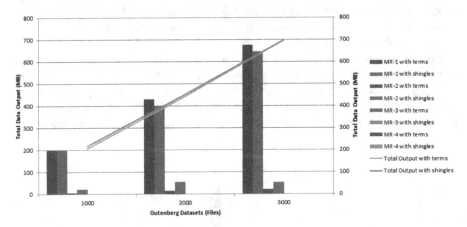

Fig. 23. The data output of 500-NN queries with terms and shingles (Color figure online)

7   Discussion

When doing experiments with terms and shingles, we observe that *Query Term Filtering* applying to terms produces less data output than that applying to shingles. In other words, the number of terms is filtered more than that of shingles in the same method. More concretely, a number of terms are approximately 1.3x as many as that of shingles on average in the filtering self-join. Nevertheless, a number of shingles are approximately 1.15x as many as that of terms on average in pivot case, approximately

1.09x as many as that of terms on average in search-by-example, and approximately 1.03x as many as that of terms on average in 500-NN queries. As a consequence, these numbers indicate that *Query Term Filtering* works with terms more effectively than it does with shingles, which results in better performance. The main reason might come from the unique characteristic of using shingles. It is worth noting that shingles generated by continuous terms bound by the length of K. Thus, the collision of two random shingles is often smaller while there is a high probability of collision for two random terms in the corpus. Because of this, the number of terms that might be shared in the query is large whilst that of shingles that might be included in the query is small. As a result, we observe that there are more filtered terms than filtered shingles against the given query.

Besides, we further describe the important factors that most matter to achieving high performance with MapReduce in order to additionally wrap up by the experiments that have been conducted so far as follows:

- The MapReduce operations should not be too complex due to limited computing resources. Moreover, neither complicated computations nor unoptimized processing improves the performance;
- The less computations the similarity measure is, the high efficiency the whole system gets [13]. Alternatively, there are different metrics to measure how similar a pair of objects is. Nevertheless, these have their own characteristic and computing complexity. One is of choice depends on specific applications and domains due to the fact that it adds its complexity to the whole computing processes;
- Natural language processing such as filtering useless symbols is essential for the proper model of documents, which leads to effectively filtering either terms or shingles. If these special symbols are not handled properly, they might easily cause unexpected errors when we process data strings by a programming language such as Python;
- The load balancing also a big issue when we do with MapReduce, for the overall performance is always finalized by the last MapReduce job. Though some implementations of MapReduce, like Hadoop, try to distribute the work load during their execution, there is also a promising need to find out adaptive load-balancing strategies for running algorithms so that the amounts of key-value pairs output by either mappers or reducers are relatively the same among them;
- The ways of implementing Map and Reduce functions with key-value pairs also affect the entire system and its performance. Hence, an optimized execution plan is preferred;
- Depending on the characteristics of the cluster of commodity machines, the environment settings in general and the configurations in particular can be further optimized to improve the overall performance.

On the other hand, clustering techniques may be useful when being integrated into the proposed methods. The idea behind is to partition the search space into several sub-spaces in that only some spaces are promoted as candidates for similarity search. From this point of view, clustering techniques help reduce the search space. The way of clustering, however, gives big influences to the above goal. For instance, if there are a few clusters, most of unnecessary shingles will be considered and this does not help at all in comparison either with or without the simple clustering methods. Otherwise, in case there are too many clusters, extra costs from cluster checking become big and do harm to the overall performance. Thus, finding out the trade-off optimally balancing the two cases and well partitioning the search space is essentially an open research. One possible solution, in our case, comes from a family of phonetic hashing methods (e.g., Double Metaphone [15]) to strengthen the power of pivots. The basic idea is to transform the original search space into another one by grouping similar terms in writing and pronunciation. Doing by this way makes the new search space become less jumble and easily to be pruned, for most of the similar terms belong to the same cluster. On the other side, one-way hashing functions should be optionally used not only to support the clustering process but also to help reduce the size of k-shingles when the k parameter is large. Using this way aims at saving data transferred throughout the network and written into the distributed file system. Last but not least, one-way hashing functions enhance data security, for real text data as well as query data should not be revealed in the time of similarity search.

Other problems from our research work are also how to assure data quality as well as data freshness. They require much effort on many intensive tasks to pre-process data before feeding MapReduce operations. Normally, an update policy may be alternatively set up when running MapReduce-1 operations by either automatically done in a period of time or manually executed on request. Additionally, other similarity measures or variants of simple forms such as Cosine, Dice, edit distance, or Hamming distance [17, 18], and similarity computing methods like locality-sensitive hashing [20, 21] should also be seriously considered when extracting similarity scores due to the fact that the unique characteristics of application domains and similarity measures, themselves, may prefer different optimizations. For instance, the research studies in [13, 14] show that doing MapReduce-based similarity search with Jaccard outperforms that with Cosine. The reason is that Cosine measure demands more computations to normalize the weights of documents, which adds more overheads in terms of performance and data volume.

Moreover, approximate searches should be a shining point when integrated into our methods in order to further improve the overall performance whilst keeping trying ensuring the accuracy of the results. Furthermore, it would be great if the proposed methods can adapt to other well-known similarity search cases such as pairwise similarity and similarity joins. Last but not least, doing more comparisons with state-of-the-art helps consolidate and enhance our methods. These matters above are then left as our future work.

8 Summary

In this paper, we propose an adaptive similarity search scheme supporting large-scale processing with MapReduce in massive datasets. In addition, we equip our proposed scheme with collaborative strategic refinements that not only promote the potential scalability of MapReduce paradigm but also eliminate unnecessary computations as well as diminish candidate sizes. Besides, our proposed methods are flexibly adaptable to popular similarity search cases such as pairwise similarity, search-by-example, range queries, and k-NN queries. Moreover, these methods are verified by many empirical experiments on real datasets and experienced with Hadoop framework, which is deployed in the commodity machines. Furthermore, we model our documents with distinct n-grams known as shingles, together with terms representation, so that we observe the difference between them from the proposed methods. Last but not least, we discuss other challenges as our future work under the context of big data, together with other open research issues, in order to further strengthen and enhance our methods supporting data-intensive applications.

Acknowledgements. We would like to give our thanks to Mr. Faruk Kujundžić, Information Management team, Johannes Kepler University Linz, for kindly supporting us in Alex Cluster.

References

1. Alabduljalil, M.A., Tang, X., Yang, T.: Optimizing parallel algorithms for all pairs similarity search. In: Proceedings of the 6th ACM International Conference on Web Search and Data Mining, USA, pp. 203–212 (2013)
2. Alex cluster. http://www.jku.at/content/e213/e174/e167/e186534. Accessed 4 Feb 2014
3. Apache Software Foundation: Hadoop: A Framework for Running Applications on Large Clusters Built of Commodity Hardware (2006)
4. Baraglia, R., De Francisci Morales, G., Lucchese, C.: Document similarity self-join with MapReduce. In: Proceedings of the 10th IEEE International Conference on Data Mining, pp. 731–736 (2010)
5. Dang, T.K., Küng, J.: The SH-tree: a super hybrid index structure for multidimensional data. In: Mayr, H.C., Lazanský, J., Quirchmayr, G., Vogel, P. (eds.) DEXA 2001. LNCS, vol. 2113, pp. 340–349. Springer, Heidelberg (2001)
6. Dang, T.K.: Solving approximate similarity queries. Int. J. Comput. Syst. Sci. Eng. **22**(1–2), 71–89 (2007). CRL Publishing Ltd., UK
7. DBLP data set. http://dblp.uni-trier.de/xml/. Accessed 8 Mar 2014
8. De Francisci Morales, G., Lucchese, C., Baraglia, R.: Scaling out all pairs similarity search with MapReduce. In: Proceedings of the 8th Workshop on Large-Scale Distributed Systems for Information Retrieval, pp. 25–30 (2010)
9. Dean, J., Ghemawat, S.: MapReduce: simplified data processing on large clusters. In: Proceedings of the 6th Symposium on Operating Systems Design and Implementation, pp. 137–150. USENIX Association (2004)
10. Elsayed, T., Lin, J., Oard, D.W.: Pairwise document similarity in large collections with MapReduce. In: Proceedings of the 46th Annual Meeting of the Association for Computational Linguistics on Human Language Technologies, Companion Volume, Columbus, Ohio, pp. 265–268 (2008)
11. Fenz, D., Lange, D., Rheinländer, A., Naumann, F., Leser, U.: Efficient similarity search in very large string sets. In: Ailamaki, A., Bowers, S. (eds.) SSDBM 2012. LNCS, vol. 7338, pp. 262–279. Springer, Heidelberg (2012)
12. Li, R., Ju, L., Peng, Z., Yu, Z., Wang, C.: Batch text similarity search with MapReduce. In: Du, X., Fan, W., Wang, J., Peng, Z., Sharaf, M.A. (eds.) APWeb 2011. LNCS, vol. 6612, pp. 412–423. Springer, Heidelberg (2011)

13. Phan, T.N., Küng, J., Dang, T.K.: An elastic approximate similarity search in very large datasets with MapReduce. In: Hameurlain, A., Dang, T.K., Morvan, F. (eds.) Globe 2014. LNCS, vol. 8648, pp. 49–60. Springer, Heidelberg (2014)
14. Phan, T.N., Küng, J., Dang, T.K.: An efficient similarity search in large data collections with MapReduce. In: Dang, T.K., Wagner, R., Neuhold, E., Takizawa, M., Küng, J., Thoai, N. (eds.) FDSE 2014. LNCS, vol. 8860, pp. 44–57. Springer, Heidelberg (2014)
15. Philips, L.: The double metaphone search algorithm. C/C++ Users J. **18**(6), 38–43 (2000)
16. Project Gutenberg. http://www.gutenberg.org/. Accessed 8 Mar 2014
17. Rajaraman, A., Ullman J.D.: Finding similar items. In: The book Mining of Massive Datasets, 1st edn., pp. 71–127. Cambridge University Press (2011). Chapter 3
18. Rong, C., Lu, W., Wang, X., Du, X., Chen, Y., Tung, A.K.H.: Efficient and scalable processing of string similarity join. IEEE Trans. Knowl. Data Eng. **25**(10), 2217–2230 (2013)
19. Szmit, R.: Locality sensitive hashing for similarity search using MapReduce on large scale data. In: Kłopotek, M.A., Koronacki, J., Marciniak, M., Mykowiecka, A., Wierzchoń, S.T. (eds.) IIS 2013. LNCS, vol. 7912, pp. 171–178. Springer, Heidelberg (2013)
20. Theobald, M., Siddharth, J., Paepcke, A.: Spotsigs: robust and efficient near duplicate detection in large web collections. In: Proceedings of the 31st Annual International ACM SIGIR Conference on Research and Development in Information Retrieval, pp. 563–570 (2008)
21. Ture, F., Elsayed, T., Lin, J.: No free lunch: brute force vs. locality-sensitive hashing for cross-lingual pairwise similarity. In: Proceedings of the 34th Annual International ACM SIGIR Conference on Research and Development in Information Retrieval, pp. 943–952 (2011)
22. Vernica, R., Carey, M.J., Li, C.: Efficient parallel set-similarity joins using MapReduce. In: Proceedings of the 2010 ACM SIGMOD International Conference on Management of Data, USA, pp. 495–506 (2010)
23. Xiao, C., Wang, W., Lin, X., Yu, J.X.: Efficient similarity joins for near duplicate detection. In: Proceedings of the 17th International World Wide Web Conference, pp. 131–140 (2008)
24. Zhang, D., Yang, G., Hu, Y., Jin, Z., Cai, D., He, X.: A unified approximate nearest neighbor search scheme by combining data structure and hashing. In: Proceedings of the 23rd International Joint Conference on Artificial Intelligence, pp. 681–687 (2013)

Semantic Attack on Anonymised Transactions

Jianhua Shao$^{(\boxtimes)}$ and Hoang Ong

School of Computer Science and Informatics, Cardiff University, Cardiff, UK
ShaoJ@cardiff.ac.uk

Abstract. A transaction is a data record that contains items associated with an individual. For example, a set of movies rated by an individual form a transaction. Transaction data are important to applications such as marketing analysis and medical studies, but they may contain sensitive information about individuals which must be sanitised before being used. One popular approach to anonymising transaction data is set-based generalisation, which attempts to hide an original item by replacing it with a set of items. In this paper, we study how well this method can protect transaction data. We propose an attack that aims to reconstruct original transaction data from its set-generalised version by analysing semantic relationships that exist among the items. Our experiments show that set-based generalisation may not provide adequate protection for transaction data, and about 50 % of the items added to the transactions during generalisation can be detected by our method with a precision greater than 80 %.

Keywords: Data privacy · Semantic attack · Transaction data

1 Introduction

Transaction data are records that contain items about individuals. For example, Fig. 1 shows a set of 4 transactions, each recording a set of medical conditions associated with a patient. TID is a transaction identifier which is included here for reference only; it is not part of the data.

TID	Items
1	gastric, ulcer, acid, bacteria
2	cancer, moles, bleeding, cough, bowels
3	diabetes, glucose, tiredness, itching, blurred vision
4	kidney disease, swelling, urination

Fig. 1. An Example of Transaction Data

Transaction data are important to applications such as marketing analysis and medical studies. However, such data can contain personal information which

© Springer-Verlag Berlin Heidelberg 2016
A. Hameurlain et al. (Eds.): TLDKS XXIII, LNCS 9480, pp. 75–99, 2016.
DOI: 10.1007/978-3-662-49175-1_4

must be sanitised before being used. Unfortunately, simply removing identifying items such as names or telephone numbers is not sufficient to protect transactions, because combinations of other items in a transaction may still be used to identify an individual or reveal sensitive information associated with them [27]. For example, knowing that Mary is in the dataset and has an *ulcer* will be enough to link her to T1 in Fig. 1, thereby revealing her identity within the dataset and disclosing other information about her.

A number of methods have been proposed to protect transaction data against this type of privacy disclosure, including generalisation [9, 15, 24, 28], suppression [15, 24], bucketisation [12, 26, 31] and perturbation [4, 16, 17]. One popular method is set-based generalisation, where an original item in a transaction is replaced by a set of items. This is to ensure that combinations of certain items (which an adversary may use to attack the data) will not appear infrequently in the released dataset. For example, Fig. 2 is a set-generalised version of Fig. 1 where items in brackets are generalised items. As individual items are turned into common sets by the generalisation, knowing that Mary has an *ulcer* will no longer be enough to link her to T1 with certainty in Fig. 2. This provides protection for Mary's identity and privacy.

TID	Items
1	gastric, (*ulcer, moles, glucose*), (*itching, acid, bleeding*), (*swelling, bacteria, tiredness*)
2	cancer, (*ulcer, moles, glucose*), (*itching, acid, bleeding*), cough, bowels
3	diabetes, (*ulcer, moles, glucose*), (*swelling, bacteria, tiredness*), (*itching, acid, bleeding*), blurred vision
4	kidney disease, (*swelling, bacteria, tiredness*), urination

Fig. 2. Set-Based Generalisation

However, set-based generalisation is largely a syntactic method. It works on an implicit assumption that items are contextless or even meaningless literals, and it does not take the whole transaction into account when forming a generalising set. This makes it vulnerable to semantic attacks. For example, consider the generalised items in Fig. 2 again. Although (*ulcer, moles, glucose*) in T1 suggests that Mary could have *ulcer, moles, glucose* or any combination of them, the presence of *gastric* implies that it is more likely to be *ulcer*. This type of semantic analysis will allow an adversary to reduce a generalised item to its original form, thereby breaking protection for privacy.

In the paper, we study how well transaction data can be protected by set-based generalisation. More specifically,

- We propose an attack that aims to reconstruct original transaction data from their set-generalised version by analysing semantic relationships that exist among the items. This is in contrast to other studies on quantifying privacy risk involved in publishing transaction data, where an adversary is assumed either to have de-identified but not anonymised data to attack [7,22], or to have some auxiliary information about original data available [11]. We attack anonymised transactions and require no additional information apart from the released data. Thus, our attack represents a realistic assessment of privacy risk associated with set-based generalisation.

– To determine semantic relationship among data items, we build our work on a measure called Normalised Google Distance [5]. This measure establishes semantic relationship between two terms by querying the Google repository of WWW pages: the more pages in which the two terms appear together, the more related they are considered to be. This eliminates the need to construct a single comprehensive dictionary or corpus for testing term relationships and ensures that our approach is generic and practical.

Our experiments on real-world datasets show that set-based generalisation may not provide adequate protection for transaction data, and about 50 % of the items added to transactions during generalisation can be detected by our method with a precision greater than 80 %. This is significant as it suggests that by using semantic relationship, it is highly likely that items added into a transaction as a cover by the generalisation process may be eliminated by an adversary and original transactions may be reconstructed. As our approach uses information that is readily available from the released data and Google, the privacy risks identified in this paper are real.

The rest of the paper is organised as follows. Section 2 reviews the related work. Section 3 provides concepts and notations necessary to understanding the proposed approach. In Sect. 4, we describe the three key steps of our de-anonymisation approach in detail. We report experimental results in Sect. 5. Finally, Sect. 6 concludes the paper.

2   Related Work

Privacy risks associated with data publishing have been studied extensively in recent years, which has led to a range of possible attacks on released data being identified. In this section we give a brief overview of these attacks. We first introduce those that attempt to identify individuals and the sensitive information associated with them from published data directly. Then we review the attacks which aim to reconstruct original data from anonymised ones.

2.1   Identification Attacks

It has been well recognised that if some items or combinations of items appear infrequently within a dataset, then such data may be used by an adversary to identify an individual contained in the dataset. For example, Sweeney [25] considered link attack where an adversary may use so-called quasi-identifiers such as postcode, gender and age to identify an individual. Machanavajjhala et al. [21] introduced homogeneity attack which can reveal the sensitive information associated with an individual without having to identify the individual first. Li et al. [19] suggested a distribution based attack where an adversary obtains sensitive information about an individual by observing the difference between distributions of sensitive values in the original and released datasets. Narayanan and Shmatikov [22] specifically considered the identification of individuals from transactions. They assume that data are de-identified (i.e. having identifying items such as names removed), and that an adversary has some auxiliary information (i.e. knowing that several items are associated with an individual) when attacking the data. All these attacks rely on the frequency or distribution of data items in a dataset to identify individuals, and to protect data against these attacks, low frequency items are often generalised or suppressed. In contrast, we analyse semantic relationships that exist among the items and attempt to recover original data from generalised ones.

Other identification attacks assume that an adversary possesses additional knowledge beyond the data about individuals in the released data. Wong et al. [29] introduced minimality attack: if an adversary knows that data has been generalised only to meet the minimum protection requirement, then that knowledge can be used to identify an individual. Xiao et al. [32] proposed transparency attack which assumes that the adversary knows the algorithm that has been used to sanitise the data, and uses this knowledge to uncover sensitive information about individuals. Inference attack has also been studied, where data analysis techniques such as correlation analysis [18] or data mining [8] are used to discover sensitive information or patterns about individuals from de-identified or sanitised data. While these attacks go beyond data frequency analysis and explore relationships among data or between data and anonymisation processes, they do not consider the type of semantic relationship that we consider in this paper.

2.2   Reconstruction Attacks

Reconstruction attacks do not attempt to identify individuals from published datasets directly, but instead they consider how original data may be recovered from sanitised ones. For example, when a set of data is transformed to protect privacy but the transformed dataset preserves Euclidean distances in order to support certain analytic studies, an adversary may break the transformation and recover the original values by using a few known data points in the dataset [11]. Once the original data have been reconstructed, the privacy is deemed to be broken and individuals may be identified using the identification attacks discussed above. The majority of studies in this area have been carried out for statistic data releasing [13, 16]. Common techniques analyse correlations and distributions in data perturbed through noise addition [1] or data swapping [6]. In contrast, we consider set-generalised data and analyse semantic relationships among the data items, rather than relying on certain statistic properties that are assumed to be preserved in the released data. Moreover, we do not require any prior knowledge about the data, and rely on the released data only.

Anandan and Clifton studied how a sanitised term in a text may be re-identified based on its semantic relationships with others [2]. They assume that the term is generalised according to a specific taxonomy, and they measure its semantic relationships with others w.r.t. this taxonomy in order to re-identify it. In so doing, they rely on the existence of a taxonomy for semantic analysis, which is not entirely realistic in practice. Sánchez and Rovira [23], on the other hand, considered the possibility of uncovering a suppressed term from a sanitised text without using a taxonomy. Similar to our work, they use Normalised Google Distance to measure semantic relationships among the terms. While we share the view that semantic relationships among terms must be taken into account when anonymising data and the Normalised Google Distance is a practical way to analyse their relationships, our work has a different focus from theirs. Given a sensitive term, Sánchez and Rovira apply semantic analysis *before* anonymisation to assess whether it is sufficient to suppress this term only or other terms must also be suppressed in order to protect it. In contrast, we apply semantic analysis *after* anonymisation, i.e., attempting to reduce a set-generalised item to its original form.

3   Preliminaries

In this section, we present some notations and concepts necessary to under-standing our approach. Let $\mathcal{I} = \{i_1, ..., i_m\}$ be a finite set of literals called *items*. A *transaction* T over $\mathcal{I}$ is a set of items $T = \langle a_1, a_2, \ldots, a_k \rangle$, where each $a_j, 1 \leq j \leq k$ is a distinct item in $\mathcal{I}$. A transaction dataset $\mathcal{D} = \{T_1, ..., T_n\}$ is a set of transactions over $\mathcal{I}$.

Definition 1 (Itemset and Support). *Any subset $I \subseteq \mathcal{I}$ is called an* itemset. *An itemset I is supported by transaction T if $I \subseteq T$. We use $\sigma(I, \mathcal{D})$ to represent the number of transactions in $\mathcal{D}$ that support I, and we call these transactions supporting transactions of I in $\mathcal{D}$.*

For example, $\langle$gastric, ulcer, acid, bacteria$\rangle$ is a transaction in Fig. 1. $\langle$gastric, ulcer$\rangle$ is an itemset and is supported by T1, hence has the support of $\sigma(\langle$gastric, ulcer$\rangle, \mathcal{D}) = 1$. T1 is its supporting transaction.

When the support for an itemset is low, i.e. the itemset appeared infrequently within a transaction dataset, an attacker may use it to identify an individual with a high probability. A popular approach to ensuring that such itemsets would not compromise privacy is set-based generalisation [20], where individual items are replaced by a set of items.

Definition 2 (Set-Based Generalisation). *A set-based generalisation is a partition $\tilde{\mathcal{I}}$ of $\mathcal{I}$ in which each item $i \in \mathcal{I}$ is replaced by the partition to which it belongs. Each partition is called a* generalised item, *and each i is mapped to its generalised version $\tilde{i}$ using a generalisation function $\Phi : \mathcal{I} \rightarrow \tilde{\mathcal{I}}$. When an item is generalised to itself, we say that the item is* trivially generalised.

We denote a generalised item by listing its items in brackets, e.g. (*ulcer*, *moles*, *glucose*) in Fig. 2 is a generalised item, and we interpret a generalised item as representing any non-empty subset of its member items, e.g. (*ulcer*, *moles*, *glucose*) may represent *ulcer*, *moles*, *glucose* or any combination of them. Generalisation can help prevent identity disclosure as it increases the number of transactions in the dataset that may be linked to an individual through combinations of items [20]. For example, consider the mapping of item *swelling* in Fig. 1 to the generalised item (*swelling*, *bacteria*, *tiredness*) in Fig. 2. (*swelling*, *bacteria*, *tiredness*) is supported by 3 transactions in Fig. 2, whereas *swelling* is only supported by 1 transaction in Fig. 1.

Various privacy models have been proposed and they require different privacy constraints to be satisfied by the released data [10,20,27,33]. For the purpose of this paper, we use a simple, but commonly adopted privacy protection model, based on support count.

Definition 3 (Protected Transactions). *Let $\tilde{\mathcal{D}} = \{\tilde{T}_1, \tilde{T}_2, \ldots, \tilde{T}_n, \}$ be a set of set-generalised transactions, and $p = (I, \sigma_{min})$ be a privacy constraint that requires an itemset I to have a minimum support of σ_{min} in $\tilde{\mathcal{D}}$. $\tilde{\mathcal{D}}$ is protected w.r.t. p if either $\sigma(I, \tilde{\mathcal{D}}) \geq \sigma_{min}$ or $\sigma(I, \tilde{\mathcal{D}}) = 0$.*

Given a set of protected transactions w.r.t. a set of privacy constraints, we are interested to see if any constraint may be "violated" by performing some semantic analysis on the published (set-generalised) data. That is, we are interested to know if some items in a generalised item could be removed based on their semantic relationships with other items in a transaction, thereby reducing the extent of generalisation and recovering some low frequency itemsets from the published transactions.

4   Context Based Semantic Attack

In this section we describe our proposed semantic attack. Given a generalised item $\tilde{i} = (\hat{i}_1, \hat{i}_2, \ldots, \hat{i}_s)$, where each $\hat{i}_j$, $1 \leq j \leq s$ is either an original item or a non-original item that has been added to the transaction by the anonymisation process to provide a cover for the original items, our goal is to identify and remove non-original items from $\tilde{i}$ based on semantic analysis. Our approach is outlined in Fig. 3, which takes any set-generalised transactions as input, and produces a de-anonymised dataset with as many non-original items removed from generalised items as possible as output. In the following sections we describe the three key steps of our approach, *context extraction*, *scoring* and *elimination*, in detail.

4.1   Context Extraction

We consider items in a transaction to have some semantic relationships between them. That is, we would expect items in a transaction to occur in a coherent manner. For example, items in transaction ⟨gastric, ulcer, acid, bacteria⟩ in Fig. 1 are all related to a particular medical diagnosis, and one would not expect

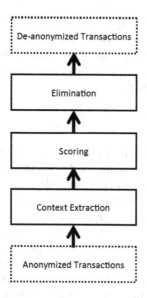

Fig. 3. Context Based Semantic Attack

to see item *sky*, for instance, to occur in it. Thus, items in a transaction can be seen as collectively forming a *context* for the transaction, which can be used to judge if it is plausible for a particular item to occur in the transaction. Our approach is based on this observation, and our first step is to extract a suitable context from a transaction.

Definition 4 (Transaction Context). *Given a generalised transaction $\tilde{T}$, $C \subset \tilde{T}$ is a context of $\tilde{T}$, if each item $i_k \in C$, $0 \leq k \leq |C|$ is trivially generalised. We call an item in C a contextual item.*

Note that only original items can be used to form a context. This is because generalised items may contain items added by the anonymisation process, therefore they may not provide reliable contextual information for the transaction. Given a generalised transaction, many contexts may be formed. However, a large C is not desirable. This is because a large transaction (hence the possibility of a large context) may contain multiple contexts. For example, a patient discharge report may contain the diagnoses of several diseases that the patient has. Using too many contextual items could confuse semantic analysis and result in wrong estimation of semantic relationships. Moreover, it will incur substantial computation as semantic relationships between generalised items and each contextual item need to be analysed. This implies a large number of queries to Google which is time consuming.

In our work, therefore, we extract only the neighbouring items to a generalised item to form a context. For example, given transaction ⟨kidney disease, (swelling, bacteria, tiredness), urination⟩ in Fig. 2, we use *kidney disease* and *urination* as contextual items for generalised item (*swelling, bacteria, tiredness*). For simplicity of discussion in this paper we assume that there is at least one trivially generalised item in a generalised transaction $\tilde{T}$. If no trivially generalised items available in a generalised transaction, then items in other generalised items may be used as contextual items. Detailed discussion on how this may be done is beyond the scope of this paper.

4.2   Scoring

The scoring step is to establish relationships between items in a generalised item and the transaction's contextual items. For example, in Fig. 2, to identify any non-original items from generalised item (*ulcer, moles, glucose*) using *gastric* as a context, the scoring step will measure semantic relationship between every item in (*ulcer, moles, glucose*) and item *gastric*.

One approach to measuring how a given pair of items is related is to use an expert-specified ontology, such as the Wordnet [3]. Ontologies provide hierarchies of concepts and allow class inclusion or subsumption to be inferred, thus can help determine if the two items are related conceptually. However, such measures are not suitable for our purpose because they tend to measure similarity rather than relatedness, and they do not take different contexts into account. For example, "string" and "cord" may be deemed similar by an ontology when they are both taken to mean a thin rope, but it does not suggest if these two terms are likely to be used together, nor they actually represent similar concepts if we consider the use of the two terms in a programming context.

An alternative approach is to use a corpus of texts, and the relatedness of two items is judged by how they appear together within the corpus of texts [14]. This can help establish term relatedness based on how they are actually used in a context, rather than just if the terms are conceptually similar. However, this approach needs to construct a comprehensive and unbiased corpus for testing the usage of any terms, and this is not always feasible in practice.

In this paper, we follow the corpus based approach, but to avoid the need to construct a comprehensive corpus, we adopt the *Normalised Google Distance* (NGD) [5] measure which considers the entire world-wide-web as a corpus. Given two terms x and y, their semantic relatedness is established by

$$NGD(x,y) = \frac{max(\log f(x), \log f(y)) - \log f(x,y)}{\log(N) - min(\log f(x), \log f(y))} \tag{1}$$

where $f(x)$ denotes the number of Google pages containing x, $f(y)$ the number of pages containing y, $f(x,y)$ the number of pages containing both x and y, and N is the total number of pages Google has in its repository. The lower the NGD score is, the more closely related the two terms are considered to be. For example, we have $NGD(\text{"paracetamol"}, \text{"HIV"}) > NGD(\text{"paracetamol"}, \text{"Cold"})$, which suggests that in general Paracetamol is more likely to be associated with Cold than with HIV.

Given a generalised transaction, we may have a number of contextual items available, and any subset of these context items may be used to attack a given generalised item. Let C be a set of contextual items used in attacking a generalised item $\tilde{i}_j$ and $\hat{i}$ be an item in $\tilde{i}_j$. We measure semantic relatedness between $\hat{i}$ and C by

$$d_{C,\hat{i}} = \frac{\sum_{j \in C} NGD(j, \hat{i})}{|C|}$$

where $|C|$ is the number of contextual items in C. That is, when multiple contextual items are used, an average score between $\hat{i}$ and its context set C is used as a measure of how likely $\hat{i}$ belongs to the transaction. For example, given $\tilde{T} = \langle i_1, i_2, i_3, (i_7, i_8), i_4, i_5, i_6 \rangle$, the semantic relatedness between i_7 and its context $C = \{i_3, i_4\}$ is measured by $d_{C,i_7} = (NGD(i_3, i_7) + NGD(i_4, i_7))/2$.

One requirement of set-based generalisation is that generalised items form k-equivalence groups. That is, each generalised item will appear at least k times within the released transactions. This is to ensure that the probability of using generalised items to link an individual to a transaction is no more than $1/k$. Therefore, when attacking a generalised item $\tilde{i} = (\hat{i}_1, \hat{i}_2, \ldots, \hat{i}_s)$, we consider the whole equivalence group together by performing NGD scoring on each occurrence of $\tilde{i}$ in different transactions and record the result in a distance table: (Fig. 4)

	$\hat{i}_1$	...	$\hat{i}_s$
C_1	$d_{C_1,\hat{i}_1}$	...	$d_{C_1,\hat{i}_s}$
...	...	...	...
C_k	$d_{C_k,\hat{i}_1}$	...	$d_{C_k,\hat{i}_s}$

Fig. 4. Distance Table

where columns are items in the generalised item under attack, and rows are contextual items selected from each transaction in the equivalence group to attack the generalised item. Note that while the generalised item $\tilde{i}$ is identical in every transaction within the equivalence group, the contextual items that are selected and used to attack it need not to be the same. In fact, as each transaction is different and contexts are likely to be different, thereby allowing the membership of $\hat{i}$ in $\tilde{i}$ to be discriminated in a given transaction. For example, applying our scoring function to the generalised item $(ulcer, moles, glucose)$ in Fig. 2 using C_1, C_2 and C_3 as contexts, we obtain the distance table in Fig. 5.

	ulcer	moles	glucose
$C_1 = \{gastric\}$	0.87	0.77	1.17
$C_2 = \{cancer\}$	1.02	1.45	0.85
$C_3 = \{diabetes\}$	1.11	1.98	0.73

Fig. 5. An Example Distance Table

This generalised item contains 3 items and forms a 3-equivalence group, therefore the distance tables has 3 columns and 3 rows. The largest distance is 1.98 between *moles* and *diabetes*, suggesting that they are not as related as others are, hence *moles* is likely to be an item introduced into T3 by the generalisation process, rather than an original item in T3. Note that in this example, we used a single contextual item to attack the generalised item. In general, any number of contextual items may be used if they are available.

4.3   Elimination

Elimination is a step that applies a set of criteria to eliminate non-original items from a distance table, based on the scores obtained from the scoring step. This corresponds to eliminating items which are less related to the context of a transaction. Once the semantic relatedness between the contextual items and the items in a generalised item is established, we employ some heuristics to eliminate those that are deemed to be not belonging to the original transactions from the generalised items. In the following sections, we give some heuristic methods to find such items.

Maximum Distance Attack (MDA). Given a distance table for an equivalence group of k transactions and an generalised item, it is easy to see from the definition of set-based generalisation that there exists at least one item that does not belong to the original transactions. So a conservative method is to consider the one with the greatest value in the distance table to be that item, and eliminate it from the generalised item. That is, we have

$$\mathbb{D}_e = \mathbb{D} \setminus \max(\mathbb{D})$$

where $\max(\mathbb{D})$ is the greatest value in the distance table $\mathbb{D}$. For example, applying this method to Fig. 5, we eliminate *moles* from T3 (distance values in bold indicate original items): (Fig. 6)

	ulcer	moles	glucose
$C_1 = \{gastric\}$	**0.87**	0.77	1.17
$C_2 = \{cancer\}$	1.02	**1.45**	0.85
$C_3 = \{diabetes\}$	1.11	-	**0.73**

Fig. 6. An Example of MDA

The resultant de-anonymised transactions are shown in Fig. 7. The data is no longer considered to offer sufficient protection for privacy, because with the de-anonymised dataset, if an adversary knows that an individual has *moles*, he or she can link this individual to a specific transaction in the dataset with a probability of 1/2, which is higher than the 1/3 offered by the anonymised data.

TID	Items
1	gastric, (**ulcer**, *moles, glucose*), (*itching*, **acid**, *bleeding*), (*swelling*, **bacteria**, *tiredness*)
2	cancer, (*ulcer*, **moles**, *glucose*), (*itching, acid*, **bleeding**), cough, bowels
3	diabetes, (*ulcer*, ~~moles~~, **glucose**), (*swelling, bacteria*, **tiredness**), (**itching**, *acid, bleeding*), blurred vision
4	kidney disease, (**swelling**, *bacteria, tiredness*), urination

Fig. 7. De-anonymised Fig. 2 Following MDA

Threshold Distance Attack (TDA). MDA is however very conservative, and it does not attempt to eliminate all possible non-original items from a generalised item. A more aggressive attack could consider all items with a distance above a certain threshold to be non-original, therefore eliminate them all from the generalised item. That is, given a parameter δ and a distance table, we perform the following as long as d is not the last item left in a column or row in $\mathbb{D}$:

$$\mathbb{D}_e = \mathbb{D} \setminus \bigcup_{d \in \mathbb{D}, d > \delta} d$$

The method is given in Algorithm 1, which checks if each distance value is above a threshold δ and eliminates it if it is. In this paper, we use the average distance in $\mathbb{D}$ as δ:

$$\delta = \frac{\sum_{d \in \mathbb{D}} d}{|\mathbb{D}|}$$

where $|\mathbb{D}|$ is the number of items in $\mathbb{D}$.

Algorithm 1. *Threshold Distance Attack ($\mathbb{D}, \delta$)*

Input: Distance table $\mathbb{D}$ and threshold value δ
Output: De-anonymised distance table $\mathbb{D}_e$
1: $\mathbb{D}_s = \emptyset$
2: **for** $\alpha_{ij} \in \mathbb{D}$ **do**
3:     **if** $\alpha_{ij} > \delta$ **then**
4:         $\mathbb{D}_s \leftarrow \alpha_{ij}$
5:     **end if**
6: **end for**
7: **return** $\mathbb{D}_e = \mathbb{D} \setminus \mathbb{D}_s$

For example, the average distance in Fig. 5 is 1.11. Eliminating items with a distance greater than this threshold from Fig. 5 we obtain Fig. 8. Note that while this method has eliminated more non-original items than MDA did from generalised items, it has also eliminated a wrong one. For brevity of presentation, we will not give the de-anonymised transactions themselves hereafter as they are obvious from the final distance table.

	ulcer	moles	glucose
$C_1 = \{gastric\}$	**0.87**	0.77	-
$C_2 = \{cancer\}$	1.02	-	0.85
$C_3 = \{diabetes\}$	1.11	-	**0.73**

Fig. 8. An Example of TBA

The effectiveness of TDA however depends on the amount of original items in generalised items or equivalently in a distance table.

Definition 5 (Density). *Given a distance table* $\mathbb{D}$ *and a set of original items* $\mathbb{D}_o \subset \mathbb{D}$, *the* density *of* $\mathbb{D}$ *is defined as:*

$$\theta = \frac{|\mathbb{D}_o|}{|\mathbb{D}|}$$

So the lower the density is, the more non-original items we have in generalised items. When the density is low, the average distance tends to be greater than those associated with original items, hence elimination tends to be more effective. We will further explore this in Sect. 5.

Weighted Distance Attack (WDA). We observe that when an item is eliminated, it should have an affect on the other items in a distance table. Intuitively, removing one item should suggest that the other items are more likely to be original. Based on this observation we propose a weighted distance attack which eliminates items from a distance table in iterations: one item is eliminated in each iteration, then the remaining distances in the table are updated w.r.t. the item that has been eliminated. This continues until no more elimination can be performed.

Observe that each row or column in a distance table always contains at least one original item. So if a row or column contains m items, we can assume that each item has at least a probability of $1/m$ to be an original one. As items are eliminated from the distance table, these probabilities will change and we use these probabilities as weights to revise the distances recorded in the distance table as follows:

Definition 6 (Weighted Distance). *Let* $\mathbb{D}$ *be a distance table and* α_{ij} *be the distance value at row* i *and column* j *in* $\mathbb{D}$. *The* weighted distance α_{ij}^w *for* α_{ij} *is calculated by*

$$\alpha_{ij}^w = \alpha_{ij} \times (1 - \frac{1}{N_r - E_r^i}) \times (1 - \frac{1}{N_c - E_c^j})$$

where N_r *and* N_c *are the number of rows and columns in* $\mathbb{D}$, *and* E_r^i *and* E_c^j *are the number of eliminated items in row* i *and column* j, *respectively.*

That is, α_{ij} is first revised by the row weights ($\frac{1}{N_r - E_r^i}$) and then by the column weights ($\frac{1}{N_c - E_c^j}$). The more items are eliminated from a row (column), the more likely the remaining items in the row (column) will be original, and revision given in Definition 6 reflects that. So unlike MDA or TDA, each elimination by WDA affects how the rest of items may be processed. Algorithm 2 shows the WDA method.

Algorithm 2. *Weighted Distance Attack* $(\mathbb{D}, N_r, N_c)$

Input: A distance table $\mathbb{D}$ with N_r rows and N_c columns
Output: De-anonymised distance table $\mathbb{D}_e$
1: $E_c, E_r \leftarrow$ initialise()
2: $\mathbb{D}^w \leftarrow \mathcal{W}(\mathbb{D}, N_r, N_c, E_r, E_c)$
3: $\delta \leftarrow \frac{\sum_{d \in \mathbb{D}^w} d}{|\mathbb{D}^w|}$
4: $m_{ij} \leftarrow \max(\mathbb{D}^w)$ if $N_r - E_r^i > 1$ and $N_c - E_c^j > 1$
5: **while** $m_{ij} > \delta$ **do**
6:     $\mathbb{D}_{ij}^w \leftarrow \emptyset$
7:     $E_r^i \leftarrow E_r^i + 1, E_c^j \leftarrow E_c^j + 1$
8:     $\mathbb{D}^w \leftarrow \mathcal{W}(\mathbb{D}, N_r, N_c, E_r, E_c)$
9:     $m_{ij} \leftarrow \max(\mathbb{D}^w)$ if $N_r - E_r^i > 1$ and $N_c - E_c^j > 1$
10: **end while**
11: **return** $\mathbb{D}^w$ as $\mathbb{D}_e$

Step 1 initialises E_r and E_c which are used to record the number of eliminations in each row and column. They help update weighted distances without having to scan the table multiple times. Step 2 calculates a weighted distance table $\mathbb{D}^w$ according to Definition 6 using Algorithm 3. A threshold δ is derived in Step 3 using the initial scores in $\mathbb{D}$. Step 4 finds the maximum score m_{ij} in $\mathbb{D}^w$ as long as it is not the last item in row i or column j. If it is greater than δ (Step 5), then m_{ij} is eliminated (set the entry in $\mathbb{D}^w$ to empty) in Step 6, and E_c and E_r are updated in Step 7. $\mathbb{D}^w$ is re-calculated and a new m_{ij} is selected in Steps 8 and 9. This continues until no distance values are above the threshold, and the resultant distance table is returned in Step 11.

As an example, consider Fig. 5 again. To start with, we assume that one item in each row and column is original and each item is equally likely to be the original item, hence we have the two initial weights tables as shown in Figs. 9(a) and (b). The entries in Fig. 5 are then revised using these two tables according to Definition 6 to produce Fig. 9(c) (contexts C_1, C_2 and C_3 refer to the same contexts as given in Fig. 8):

The elimination of an item from Fig. 9(c) is then carried out, based on the following conditions: (a) the item has the greatest distance in the table, (b) the item is not the last one in a row or column, and (c) its distance is greater than the average distance in the table. Note that in this case, the average threshold is calculated from the revised table, i.e. $\delta = 0.49$. *moles* in T3 satisfies these three conditions, hence is eliminated.

Algorithm 3. $\mathcal{W}(\mathbb{D}, N_r, N_c, E_r, E_c)$

Input: A distance table $\mathbb{D}$ with N_r rows and N_c columns, and elimination counters
    E_r and E_c
Output: A weighted distance table $\mathbb{D}^w$
1: $\mathbb{D}^w \leftarrow \emptyset$
2: **for** $i = 0$ to N_r **do**
3:    **for** $j = 0$ to N_c **do**
4:       $\mathbb{D}^w_{ij} \leftarrow \mathbb{D}_{ij} \times (1 - \frac{1}{N_r - E_r^i}) \times (1 - \frac{1}{N_c - E_c^j})$
5:    **end for**
6: **end for**
7: **return** $\mathbb{D}^w$

---

	ulcer	moles	glucose
C_1	1/3	1/3	1/3
C_2	1/3	1/3	1/3
C_3	1/3	1/3	1/3

(a) Row Weights

	ulcer	moles	glucose
C_1	1/3	1/3	1/3
C_2	1/3	1/3	1/3
C_3	1/3	1/3	1/3

(b) Column Weights

	ulcer	moles	glucose
C_1	**0.39**	0.34	0.52
C_2	0.45	**0.65**	0.38
C_3	0.49	0.88	**0.32**

(c) Weighted Table

Fig. 9. First Iteration of WDA

After *moles* is removed, the two weights tables are updated and the results are shown in Figs. 10(a) and (b). These two tables are then used to revise Fig. 5 to give Fig. 10(c):

	ulcer	moles	glucose
C_1	1/3	1/3	1/3
C_2	1/3	1/3	1/3
C_3	1/2	-	1/2

(a) Row Weights

	ulcer	moles	glucose
C_1	1/3	1/2	1/3
C_2	1/3	1/2	1/3
C_3	1/3	-	1/3

(b) Column Weights

	ulcer	moles	glucose
C_1	**0.39**	0.26	0.52
C_2	0.45	**0.48**	0.38
C_3	0.37	-	**0.24**

(c) Weighted Table

Fig. 10. Second Iteration of WDA

Following the same process, *glucose* in T1 is eliminated, and weights are updated and the weighted table is re-calculated to produce Fig. 11. Now, no more distances in Fig. 11(c) are above the threshold, so the elimination process terminates. It is interesting to compare the result to that obtained using MDA and TDA: it has eliminated more non-original items than MDA did, but has not wrongly eliminated *moles* from T2 as TDA did. This suggests that WDA is a more effective attacking method, and we shall further demonstrate this in Sect. 5 when we report our experimental results.

We now consider the performance of WDA in the worst case scenario, where WDA eliminates items until there is only one item left in each row and column of a distance table. In this case, the algorithm can perform maximum $N_r \times N_c - \max(N_r, N_c)$ number of iterations. In each iteration, the weight calculation

	ulcer	moles	glucose
C_1	1/2	1/2	-
C_2	1/3	1/3	1/3
C_3	1/2	-	1/2

(a) Row Weights

	ulcer	moles	glucose
C_1	1/3	1/2	-
C_2	1/3	1/2	1/2
C_3	1/3	-	1/2

(b) Column Weights

	ulcer	moles	glucose
C_1	**0.29**	0.19	-
C_2	0.45	**0.48**	0.28
C_3	0.37	-	**0.18**

(c) Weighted Table

Fig. 11. Third and Final Iteration of WDA

(Algorithm 3) requires $N_r \times N_c$ time to process. Therefore, the overall complexity of WDA is $\mathcal{O}((N_r \times N_c - \max(N_r, N_c)) \times (N_r \times N_c)) = \mathcal{O}((N_r \times N_c)^2)$. So, WDA is more expensive than TDA which has a linear cost of $\mathcal{O}(N_r \times N_c)$, as it searches through the distance table and eliminates all items having higher distances than the threshold in one pass.

4.4 Discussion

In this section we consider two further issues associated with our proposed context-based semantic attack.

Generalised Items Unmarked. The attacks we described in the previous section are based on an assumption that an adversary knows which items are generalised, so that they can identify contextual items to attack the data. This may not be the case in practice. A data publisher may not release the data with generalised items clearly marked. For example, a set of generalised transactions may be released as shown in Fig. 12.

To identify which items form a generalised item and which ones can be used as contextual items from such data, we may use the following rules:

- Any item that appears in k or more transactions is considered to be part of a generalised item, where k is a privacy requirement which we have described previously.
- Any item that appears in less than k transactions is considered to be an original item, thus may be used as a contextual item.

TID	Items
1	gastric, ulcer, moles, glucose, itching, acid, bleeding, swelling, bacteria, tiredness
2	cancer, ulcer, moles, glucose, itching, acid, bleeding, cough, bowels
3	diabetes, ulcer, moles, glucose, swelling, bacteria, tiredness, itching, acid, bleeding, blurred vision
4	kidney disease, swelling, bacteria, tiredness, urination

Fig. 12. Anonymised Transactions with Unmarked Generalised Items

Note that while it is easy to identify items appearing in at least k transactions from the released data, grouping them correctly into generalised items may not be straightforward, especially when a transaction contains more than one generalised item. This can result in a large distance table when too many items are grouped incorrectly into one generalised item, making the attacks expensive to perform, or wrong semantic relationships being estimated due to wrong items being grouped together. How to best group such items into generalised transaction needs further study, and we do not discuss this further in this paper.

Semantic Relationships among Data. The attacks we described in the previous section also assumed that semantic relationships naturally exist among the items of a transaction, which can then be used to filter out non-original items. However, this may not be the case in some applications. For example, items in a shopping basket typically form a transaction, but items in such transactions may not have the type of semantic relationship that we consider in this paper. For instance, in ⟨milk, (bread, bacon), cheese, medicine⟩, *bread* may be considered to be more likely to be an original item than *bacon* is by our methods, since it appears more frequently with *milk* and *cheese* than *bacon* does. However, this would be unjustified, as items of a transaction in this case are related more by shopping preferences, rather than by semantic relationships. Our methods are unsuitable to use to attack this type of transaction data.

5   Experiments

In this section, we report our experimental results and compare the effectiveness of our proposed methods. We first describe the datasets used in our experiments, and then compare our methods in terms recall and precision in identifying and correctly eliminating non-original items from a generalised item.

5.1   Datasets and Preparation

We used three datasets with different characteristics in our experiments. These datasets contain transactions that are extracted from i2b2 documents[1], articles from GoArticles.com[2] and AOL search query logs[3], and their characteristics are summarised in Table 1.

The AOL dataset is already in the form of transaction: each user's search session is a transaction and each searching keyword is an item in the transaction. The i2b2 transactions are extracted from documents, using the *Stanford*

---

[1] i2b2 (www.i2b2.org) is a set of de-identified notes from the Research Patient Data Repository at Partners Health Care released for a series of NLP Challenges organized by Dr. Ozlem Uzuner.

[2] The data are collected from articles at http://www.goarticles.com covering various topics.

[3] http://gregsadetsky.com/aol-data/.

Table 1. Properties of Datasets

Properties	AOL	i2b2	GoArticle
Size (No of transactions)	758	643	263
Length (items in a transaction)	1 to 5	150 to 200	150 to 200
Items to be protected	127	112	45
Original/Generalised	1/6	1/6	1/3
Quality	Few typos	Many typos and abbreviations	Content cleansed
Context	Multiple	Single (Medical)	Multiple

POS Tagger package[4]. We extract nouns and noun-phases only from the documents. Each document results in one transaction and the nouns and noun phases extracted from the document become items in the transaction. For the GoArticle dataset, we selected a set of articles that share contexts and then manually extracted terms from the articles to form transactions. All our transactions do not contain duplicated items and the order in which the terms appear in a document is preserved in the extracted transaction.

After the transactions are prepared, we anonymise them using COAT [20], a set-base generalisation method for anonymising transactions. COAT works by specifying two sets of constraints. Items to be protected form privacy constraints. In our experiments, they are randomly selected from the transactions, and the number of items selected for each dataset is given in Table 1. Items that can be used together to generalise an item form utility constraints. In our experiments we use the most general one: the entire set of items. That is, we allow any item to be used in any generalising set.

5.2 Random Attack

We compare our proposed heuristics to a baseline method which performs a random attack on generalised items. The baseline method essentially assumes that an adversary has no other information than the released dataset, and he or she can only randomly guess whether an item in a generalised item is an original one or not. There are ways that an adversary may perform a random attack:

- On each item, the adversary decides whether it should be eliminated or not. Assuming that each item is equally like to be original or introduced by the generalisation, each item has a 50 % chance to be eliminated.
- The adversary randomly picks up a random number of items to eliminate from generalised items.

We use the second method in the experiments as it allows more variation in outcome and offers better comparison for our heuristics.

---

[4] http://nlp.stanford.edu/software/tagger.shtml.

5.3   Results

We use *precision* (*p*) and *recall* (*r*) to measure how well our methods can detect non-original items correctly, and we also use the standard F-score to measure their overall quality.

$$r = \frac{\text{correct eliminations}}{\text{all non-original items}} \qquad p = \frac{\text{correct eliminations}}{\text{all eliminations}}$$

Figure 13 shows the results of our experiments. We have not included MDA as it does not attempt to remove all non-original items, hence it is not meaningful to measure its recall and compare it to other methods. In attacking a generalised item $\tilde{i}$, we use two closest items on either side of $\tilde{i}$ as contextual items. We measured recall, precision and F-score against k, the minimum size that an equivalence group must have in the released dataset. The higher the k is, the more items are likely to be added into generalised items, hence more eliminations are to be expected.

It is easy to see that TDA and WDA both outperformed the Random Attack. This suggests that semantic relationship among the items of transactions can be used to de-anonymise set-generalised transactions. This is especially so when

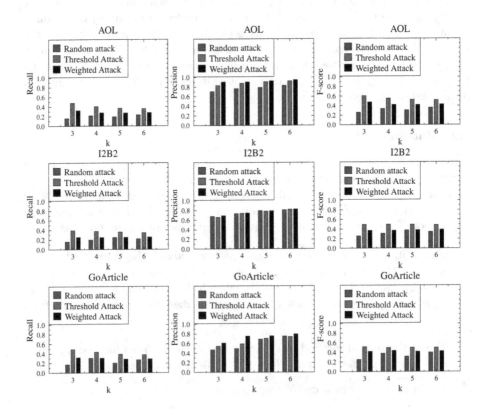

Fig. 13. Comparison of Attack Effectiveness

we deal with transactions that are extracted from text, because such extracted items (nouns and noun phrases) are often related in some context, as we have observed in our experiments. For example, about 50 % of the introduced items were removed from generalised items and precision of doing so was as high as 80 %. So transaction data sanitisation without considering semantic relationships among their items may not provide sufficient protection for individual privacy.

It is worth noting that as k increased, recall actually decreased as can be observed in Fig. 13. We attribute this to the use of thresholds in both TDA and WDA. As k increases, more non-original items are likely or needed to be added into a generalised item in order to form required equivalence groups. As a result, the average distance between the items in a generalised item and its contextual items is likely to increase, as added items are likely to be less semantically related to the contextual items. This will result in a higher threshold and a lower recall. How to set a suitable threshold needs to be investigated further.

WDA did not perform as well as TDA in terms of the overall F-score in our experiments. This is a surprise, but we believe that this is mainly due to the characteristics of the datasets used in the experiments. For all three datasets, we observed that relatively largely number of items were added into generalised items, because the data were high dimensional and sparse. This resulted in the NGD scores for the original items to be mostly below the average threshold. With TDA, this gives a very good recall (and F-score), as all the items above the threshold were removed. The Weighted Distance Attack, on the other hand, is more conservative. Anytime an item is removed, it makes the rest more likely to be original. Consequently, it eliminates less, and has a lower recall and a higher precision. This is evident from Fig. 13. To verify this, we undertook further experiments to vary the thresholds used in elimination. The result is shown in Fig. 14.

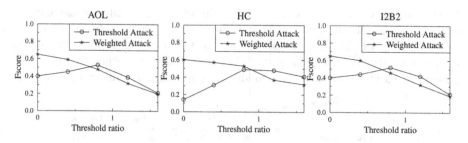

Fig. 14. Comparison of Effect of Threshold

As can be seen, when thresholds are set very low (i.e. anticipating most of the items non-original), the Weighted Distance Attack performed better. This is because as the thresholds lowered, more original items will have NGD scores that are above the threshold. They will therefore be wrongly removed by the Threshold Distance Attack, significantly reducing precision and F-score. The Weighted Distance Attack on the other hand is able to use the "enlarged" range to remove more non-original items while maintain relatively good precision due to its iterative process of elimination. This results in a better overall F-score. When the thresholds have increased to a point where it places most of the original scores below it, the threshold method works better. Again, how to find an appropriate threshold needs to be investigated further.

5.4 Effect of Data Density

As the density of a dataset is one of the important properties that can affect the performance of our methods, we study how our methods will perform with different levels of data density. To set up this experiment, we selected subsets of transactions from the datasets used in the previous experiments to have average density levels from 0.1 to 0.7.

As can be seen in Fig. 15, the precision gets lower when the density level gets higher. This is expected because when increasing the density level, less non-original items are added into generalised transactions by the process, and as our methods eliminate all possible non-original items above a fixed threshold, more wrong eliminations are likely to be made, resulting in a decreased precision. It is useful to observe that WDA has a better precision than TDA has in general and TDA's precision decreases faster than WDA does due to the use of weights. Finally, the recalls of our methods are largely unchanged with increasing density. This is because we use average distance as a criterion for eliminating items, which seems to have regulated the number of items to be removed: we observed that when less items are added into a generalised transaction in a high density dataset, less items are removed from it, resulting a relatively stable recall.

5.5 Effect of Utility Constraints

In the previous experiments, we used the most general utility constraint to anonymise a set of transactions. That is, we allow any item to be used to form a generalizing set. This helps test how our methods would perform in dealing with any utility constraint in general, but one could argue that this makes it potentially easier for an adversary to identify non-original items in a generalised

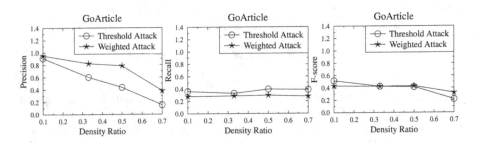

Fig. 15. Comparing Different Density Levels

item, as it is more likely for the generalisation process to introduce semantically inconsistent items into a transaction.

To test how our method would deal with more carefully constructed utility constraints, we carried out another experiment where a dataset is anonymised by more semantically consistent utility constraints. That is, we only use the items that semantically related to the item to be protected to form a generalising set during generalisation. We did this experiment with the GoArticle dataset as its multiple contexts and higher density allow us to construct some semantically very consistent utility constraints.

We used the same setup for the GoArticle dataset as in Fig. 13, except that utility constraints are constructed using the following steps:

- We first extract all the items in the dataset to form a set $\mathcal{I}$ as the domain of the dataset. We include all items so that items are less likely to be suppressed by COAT.
- Given a privacy constraint $(i_1, i_2, \ldots, i_n)$, we search all items in $\mathcal{I}$ which are semantically close to i_1. To determine the closeness of two terms i_m and i_n, we use a similarity measure given by Wu and Palmer [30] based on the WordNet ontology:

$$similarity = 2 \times depth(i_m, i_n)/(depth(i_m) + depth(i_n))$$

where $depth(i_m)$ and $depth(i_n)$ are the distances from the root to items i_m and i_n on the ontology tree, and $depth(i_m, i_n)$ is the distance from the root to the lowest common ancestor of i_m and i_n. Two terms are deemed to be sufficiently related if their similarity score is above 0.5.
- We do the same for other items in the privacy constraint. This results in a utility constraint that contains only the items that are semantically consistent with the privacy constraint. Because not all items in the domain will be added into a utility constraint, COAT may need to suppress some items in order to satisfy the privacy constraint. However, as our methods do not consider attacking suppressed items, suppressed items are ignored during attack and are not included in distance tables.

Figure 16 compares the results of attacking the same dataset anonymised using general utility constaints and semantically consistent ones. We use TDA' and WDA' to denote the results associated with the dataset that are generalised using semantically consistent utility constraints, and TDA and WDA the general ones. As can be seen, recalls associated with semantically consistent utility constraints are slightly lower as a result of introducing semantically more consistent items into transactions, resulting in a distance table with close distances, and less items are above the average distance than before. The precisions are also slightly lower because some added items are actually related to the context, causing other original items to be eliminated. This can be expected as when we add semantically similar items into a generalised item, they are also likely to be related to the context in the same way. However, the overall results in F-Score

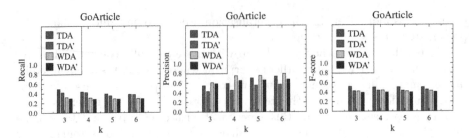

Fig. 16. Comparing General and Semantic Utility Constraints

show that our methods are not significantly affected by the types of utility constraints, hence we strongly believe that the context of transaction can be used to identify non-original items even though care has been taken to only generalise an item with semantically similar or consistent items.

5.6   Time Efficiency

Figure 17 shows the time efficiency of our methods. As the complexity of our algorithms is dependent on the size of the distance tables, we evaluate the performance of our methods by varying distance table sizes. We use $N_r \times N_r$ to denote the size of a distance table, where N_r is the number of rows and N_c is the number of columns. Timing is the time needed to attack a dataset in milliseconds.

Our experiments confirmed our analysis in Sect. 4 that TDA scales linearly, whereas WDA grows exponentially. We have not included the time taken for scoring in this experiment as the process is run remotely on the Google server and is mostly dependent on the Internet speed and external searching algorithms. But performing NGD is generally expensive. For example, in our experiment, it took more than 24 hours to run all these experiments (excluding the time that Google blocks the IP address because of mass requests to the server in a short period).

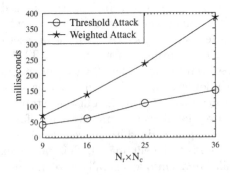

Fig. 17. Performance of attacking algorithms

6 Conclusions

In this paper, we examined if set-based generalisation can provide sufficient protection for transactions. We proposed methods which use semantic related-ness among the items to detect if certain items are unlikely to be in a gener-alised transaction. We have shown that about 50 % of the non-original items can be eliminated from generalised items with a precision greater than 80 % in our experiments. This suggests that without considering semantic relationships, anonymising transactions using set-based generalisation may not provide ade-quate protection for individual privacy. Furthermore, unlike other works, we do not assume any adversary background knowledge in attacking the data. The only information that an adversary needs in order to attack the data is the released data and Google repository. Thus, the privacy risks we identified in this paper are real.

References

1. Agrawal, R., Srikant, R.: Privacy-preserving data mining. In: Proceedings of ACM SIGMOD International Conference on Management of Data, pp. 439–450 (2000)
2. Anandan, B., Clifton, C.: Significance of term relationships on anonymization. In: IEEE/WIC/ACM International Conference on Web Intelligence and Intelligent Agent Technology (WI-IAT), pp. 253–256 (2011)
3. Budanitsky, A., Hirst, G.: Semantic distance in WordNet: an experimental, application-oriented evaluation of five measures. In: Workshop on WordNet and Other Lexical Resources, Second Meeting of the North American Chapter of the Association for Computational Linguistics, pp. 29–34 (2001)
4. Chen, K., Liu, L.: Privacy preserving data classification with rotation perturbation. In: Proceedings of IEEE International Conference on Data Mining, pp. 589–592 (2005)
5. Cilibrasi, R., Vitányi, P.: The Google similarity distance. IEEE Trans. Knowl. Data Eng. **19**(3), 370–383 (2007)
6. Dalenius, T., Reiss, S.: Data-swapping: a technique for disclosure control. J. Stat. Plann. Infer. **6**(1), 73–85 (1982)
7. Datta, A., Sharma, D., Sinha, A.: Provable De-anonymization of large datasets with sparse dimensions. In: Degano, P., Guttman, J.D. (eds.) Principles of Security and Trust. LNCS, vol. 7215, pp. 229–248. Springer, Heidelberg (2012)
8. Evfimievski, A., Gehrke, J., Srikant, R.: Limiting privacy breaches in privacy pre-serving data mining. In: Proceedings of ACM SIGMOD-SIGACT-SIGART Sym-posium on Principles of Database Systems, pp. 211–222 (2003)
9. Fung, B., Wang, K., Yu, P.: Top-down specialization for information and privacy preservation. In: Proceedings 21st International Conference on Data Engineering, pp. 205–216 (2005)
10. Ghinita, G., Tao, Y., Kalnis, P.: On the anonymization of sparse high-dimensional data. In: IEEE International Conference on Data Engineering, pp. 715–724 (2008)
11. Giannella, C.R., Liu, K., Kargupta, H.: Breaching Euclidean distance-preserving data perturbation using few known inputs. Data Knowl. Eng. **84**, 93–110 (2013)

12. He, X., Xiao, Y., Li, Y., Wang, Q., Wang, W., Shi, B.: Permutation anonymization: improving anatomy for privacy preservation in data publication. In: Proceedings of International Workshop on New Frontiers in Applied Data Mining, pp. 111–123 (2011)

13. Huang, Z., Du, W., Chen, B.: Deriving private information from randomized data. In: Proceedings of ACM SIGMOD International Conference on Management of data, pp. 37–48 (2005)

14. Islam, A., Inkpen, D.: Semantic text similarity using corpus-based word similarity and string similarity. Trans. Knowl. Discov. Data $2(2)$, 1–25 (2008)

15. Iyengar, V.S.: Transforming data to satisfy privacy constraints. In: Proceedings of ACM SIGKDD International Conference on Knowledge Discovery and Data Mining, pp. 279–288 (2002)

16. Kargupta, H., Datta, S., Wang, Q., Sivakumar, K.: On the privacy preserving properties of random data perturbation techniques. In: Proceedings of IEEE International Conference on Data Mining, pp. 99–106 (2003)

17. Kargupta, H., Datta, S., Wang, Q., Sivakumar, K.: Random-data perturbation techniques and privacy-preserving data mining. Knowl. Inform. Syst. $7(4)$, 387–414 (2004)

18. Kifer, D.: Attacks on privacy and de Finetti's theorem. In: Proceedings of ACM SIGMOD International Conference on Management of Data, pp. 127–138 (2009)

19. Li, N., Li, T., Venkatasubramanian, S.: t-Closeness: privacy beyond k-anonymity and l-diversity. In: Proceedings of IEEE International Conference on Data Engineering, pp. 106–115 (2007)

20. Loukides, G., Gkoulalas-Divanis, A., Malin, B.: COAT: constraint-based anonymization of transactions. Knowl. Inform. Syst. $28(2)$, 251–282 (2010)

21. Machanavajjhala, A., Gehrke, J., Kifer, D., Venkitasubramaniam, M.: l-Diversity: privacy beyond k-anonymity. ACM Trans. Knowl. Discov. Data 1(1) (2007)

22. Narayanan, A., Shmatikov, V.: Robust de-anonymization of large sparse datasets. In: IEEE Symposium on Security and Privacy, pp. 111–125 (2008)

23. Sánchez, D.: Detecting term relationships to improve textual document sanitization. In: Proceedings of Pacific Asia Conference on Information Systems, pp. 105–119 (2013)

24. Sweeney, L.: Achieving k-anonymity privacy protection using generalisation and suppression. Int. J. Uncertainty Fuzziness Knowl.-Based Syst. $10(5)$, 571–588 (2002)

25. Sweeney, L.: k-Anonymity: a model for protecting privacy. Int. J. Uncertainty Fuzziness Knowl.-Based Syst. $10(5)$, 557–570 (2002)

26. Terrovitis, M., Liagouris, J., Mamoulis, N., Skiadopoulos, S.: Privacy preservation by disassociation. Proc. VLDB Endowment $5(10)$, 944–955 (2012)

27. Terrovitis, M., Mamoulis, N., Kalnis, P.: Anonymity in unstructured data (2008)

28. Wang, K., Yu, P., Chakraborty, S.: Bottom-up generalization: a data mining solution to privacy protection. In: Proceedings of the 4th IEEE International Conference on Data Mining, pp. 249–256 (2004)

29. Wong, R., Fu, A., Wang, K., Pei, J.: Minimality attack in privacy preserving data publishing. In: Proceedings of the 33rd International Conference on Very Large Data Bases, pp. 543–554 (2007)

30. Wu, Z., Palmer, M.: Verbs semantics and lexical selection. In: Proceedings of the 32nd Annual Meeting on Association for Computational Linguistics, pp. 133–138 (1994)

31. Xiao, X., Tao, Y.: Anatomy: simple and effective privacy preservation. In: Proceedings of the 32nd International Conference on Very Large Data Bases, pp. 139–150 (2006)
32. Xiao, X., Tao, Y., Koudas, N.: Transparent anonymization: thwarting adversaries who know the algorithm. ACM Trans. Database Syst. 35(2) (2010)
33. Xu, Y., Fung, B., Wang, K., Fu, A., Jian, P.: Publishing sensitive transactions for itemset utility. In: Proceedings of the 8th IEEE International Conference on Data Mining, pp. 1109–1114 (2008)

Private Indexes for Mixed Encrypted Databases

Yi Tang[1,2]($\boxtimes$), Xiaolei Zhang[1,2], and Ji Zhang[1,2]

[1] School of Mathematics and Information Science,
Guangzhou University, Guangzhou 510006, China
[2] Key Laboratory of Mathematics and Interdisciplinary Sciences of Guangdong
Higher Education Institutes,
Guangzhou University, Guangzhou 510006, China
ytang@gzhu.edu.cn

Abstract. Data privacy and query performance are two closely
linked and inconsistent challenges for outsourced databases. Using
mixed encryption methods on data attributes can partially reach a
trade-off between the two challenges. However, encryption cannot
always hide the correlations between attribute values. When the
data tuples are accessed selectively, inferences based on comparing
encrypted values could be launched, and some sensitive values may
be disclosed. In this paper, we explore the intra-attribute based and
inter-attribute based inferences in mixed encrypted databases. We
develop a method to construct private indexes on encrypted values
to defend against those inferences while supporting efficient selective access to encrypted data. We have conducted some experiments
to validate our proposed method.

1 Introduction

Encryption is an essential technique for securing outsourced databases. Many
popular encryption methods such as the block ciphers and the RSA algorithm are
implemented in current programming environments and can be adopted directly
in managing outsourced data tuples. How to execute SQL queries securely and
efficiently over those encrypted data is a main challenge in database research
community, especially when the data tuples are needed to be accessed by different
users with different access rights.

Early efforts are focused on translating plain queries at trusted client side
into corresponding encrypted queries on untrusted server side and assume that
each tuple is encrypted with a single key [4,7]. This implies that all data tuples
are shared in a set of legitimate users. Access control provides users selective
rights to access data tuples. The selective encryption methods use different keys
to encrypt different data portions such as tuples or attributes [9]. To avoid users
from managing too many keys, the keys can be derived from user hierarchy
[5] and the ciphers can be changed into some other newer asymmetric methods
such as the attribute-based encryption method [17]. Although these methods can
provide an effective and possible way to combine encryption with access control,

© Springer-Verlag Berlin Heidelberg 2016
A. Hameurlain et al. (Eds.): TLDKS XXIII, LNCS 9480, pp. 100–123, 2016.
DOI: 10.1007/978-3-662-49175-1_5

the fulfillment of access control depends on the precision of locating encrypted data. It needs purified techniques to locate encrypted tuples on server side as precisely as possible.

The granularity of data encryption in outsourced databases can be a tuple or an attribute. When the encryption is on tuple level, it generally needs to introduce auxiliary attributes for indexing those attributed values involved in encrypted tuples [7], and the constructed indexes can be value-based or bucket-based [15]. It is obviously that value-based method provides more accuracies in locating encrypted tuples than the bucket-based method. Encrypting a tuple as a whole may limit the efficiency of data operation because it needs decryption before performing further data operations. Compared to the encryption in tuple, encryption on attribute level may provide more flexibilities in data operations. To meet the requirements with different data operations, an attribute value may be encrypted by mixed encryption methods. For example, in order to meet the various query requirements, an attribute value may be simultaneously encrypted by a symmetric encryption, an order preserving encryption, or a homomorphic encryption, respectively [11]. When an attribute is encrypted by mixed encryption methods, it may also require extra attributes to represent related encrypted values [14]. Note that in this case, the attribute index is value-based which can be built directly on the encrypted values.

In the scenario of outsourced databases, on one hand, the database service provider is not required to guarantee a strict separation among data portions available to different users. On the other hand, if encrypted values on some attributes cannot be distinguished on the tuples with different access control lists, the equality relations on the plain values among those tuples will be demonstrated implicitly. This may lead an adversary user draw inferences on those tuples although he has no right to access them.

In this paper, we consider the case of data encryption granularity in attributes. We will address the issue of defend against inference attacks by mitigating the explicit equality relations among attributes. We try to make a trade-off between efficient querying and selective encryption for access controls. The contributions of this paper can be enumerated as follows.

1. We explore the inferences of sensitive information due to the equality relations between encrypted attribute values.
2. We argue that the inference attacks may be not only launched on the equality relations between values of a same attribute but also on the equality relations between different attributes.
3. We introduce an encryption key constructing method which is not only depended on the key materials shared between specified users and data owners but also depended on the attribute related access control policy.

The rest of this paper is structured as follows. In Sect. 2, we first overview some encryption methods addressed in mixed encrypted databases, and then give an example to show the cases of combining access control lists with encrypted attributes. We also demonstrate possible inference attacks in those cases. In Sect. 3, we discuss the intra-attribute inference attack and the inter-attribute attack and introduce random salt to construct private indexes to defend against the inference attacks. In Sect. 4, we discuss how to define some auxiliary attributes to support the execution of SQL queries in mixed encrypted database. In Sect. 5, we give some considerations in delete, insert, and update the encrypted tuples. In Sect. 6, we propose an entropy-based measure to measure the encrypted value distribution protected in encrypted database and then propose a split strategy to defend against frequency-based linking attacks. In Sect. 7, we conduct some experiments to validate our proposed method. And finally, the conclusion is drawn in Sect. 8.

2 Background

As illustrated in Fig. 1, three parties are involved in the outsourced database scenario where the users and the proxy are on client side and a provider on server side provides outsourced database services. When user u initiates a query q_u, a proxy at client side will translate the plain q_u into an encrypted version q_u^s and send it to the remote server. After executing the query q_u^s over encrypted data on server side, the query result T_u^s will be returned to the proxy as replies. The proxy will decrypt tuples in T_u^s, perform computations over the decrypted tuples according to the conditions in q_u, and finally return results to user u. The specified user, *Administrator* (shortened as a), acts as the owner of the data. He maintains the access control lists and shares some secrets with users. He also has his own private secrets to deal with data tuples.

2.1 Encryption Methods

Encryption is the basic technique to ensure the privacy of data stored in remote database servers. Because of the randomness of encrypted data introduced by encryption methods, how to perform SQL queries over encrypted data directly in real applications becomes a hot topic in database community.

Two encryption methods, the symmetric key and the asymmetric key, are often adopted in real applications. The symmetric key encryption is traditional and uses a same key for both encryption and decryption. This key is uniquely

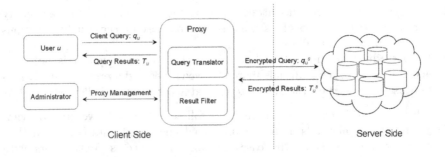

Fig. 1. The outsourced databases scenario

associated with one or more users and should be made private. The AES algorithm is a typical symmetric key encryption algorithm. When using AES cipher to encrypt a message, the ciphertext is determined by the encryption key and the initialization vector (IV). It implies that the encrypted results is deterministic when the encryption key and IV are given. In this case, the mapping between plaintext and ciphertext is injective. We label this kind of encryption as DS.

Order-preserving encryption (OP) is a kind of symmetric encryption scheme that preserves numerical ordering of plaintext. It means that $x < y \Leftrightarrow OP(x) < OP(y)$ where x and y are plain values, and $OP(x)$ and $OP(y)$ are corresponding OP-encrypted version, respectively. The OP was first suggested in [1], and was deeply studied in [2,3]. The order-preserving feature of the OP method makes it possible to perform order comparisons on encrypted data without decrypting them.

The asymmetric key encryption is another class of encryption algorithms whose keys are in pairs. This method is also known as public key cryptography, since each user will be assign with a key pair which one is made public (*the public key*) and the other secret (*the private key*). When encrypting a message with an asymmetric key encryption algorithm, a random nonce is often introduced to confuse the intermediate results. This implies that the final encrypted results are variable in different encryption procedures.

Running a database application often requires some computations on data attributes. In the case of outsourced databases, an ideal solution is to perform computations directly on encrypted data. Since homomorphic encryption (HE) enables an equivalent relation exists between one operation performed on the plaintext and another operation on the ciphertext, it is considered as an effective solution to this issue. According to the relations supported, the homomorphic encryption methods can be partially (PH) [10] or fully (FH) [6]. Considering that the current FH methods need huge space and computing cost, they are impractical in real applications. It seems that the PH methods are more practical in applications although the computations are still expensive. For example, the Paillier cryptosystem, a kind of PH method, is an additive homomorphic cryptosystem [10] which is considered as a probabilistic asymmetric encryption algorithm.

It is noted that there in fact needs a trade-off between the data privacy and query performance in outsourced databases. For example, the DS method keeps the encrypted results equality for equal original plain values, but it also introduces the equality-based inferring or frequency-based linking attacks. Making encryption keys variable could mitigate those attacks but may introduce more query computations. The OP method can be viewed as the extension of the DS method and demonstrates more performance advantages in range queries, but it leaks more relations between encrypted values. While the PH method keeps the encrypted value non-comparable, but it only benefits the computations over encrypted data and it needs other efficient ways to locate targeted encrypted tuples.

2.2   The Assumptions

In this paper, we focus on the inference attack introduced by the comparison between encrypted attribute values in different encrypted tuples. We do not consider the scenario that the attacker can undetectably corrupt the communications between clients and servers. We suppose that the communication is supported by some secure suites such as the SSL protocol. The attacker can sniffer the network traffic but cannot identify and tamper the encrypted attribute values.

We assume that the proxy is trust and secure, and the user can access any outsourced data based on his access rights. The service provider is honest but curious, sometimes a bit greedy. This means that the provider can provide the service he claims to be able to provide but he may leak some stored encrypted tuples out to others for curiosity or benefits. When no ambiguity is possible, we also call the service provider as the server.

We also assume that the encryption algorithms used in data attributes are limited in the three methods we discussed previously, i.e., the deterministic symmetric encryption DS, the order-preserving encryption method OP, and the partially homomorphic encryption method PH. Additionally, we assume that the access control policy is based on tuples.

Table 1. A Relation in plain and encrypted with ACL.

(a) Original Relation with ACL

	ACL	Sales	Inventory	ShopID
t_1	u	80	50	3
t_2	u	60	40	2
t_3	u, v	60	80	1
t_4	v	50	40	5
t_5	v, w	60	50	4

(b) Encrypted Relation with ACL-specified Mixed Encrypted Version

	tid	Sal_DS	Sal_OP	Sal_PH	Inv_DS	ShopID
t_1^s	1	$DS_u(80)$	$OP_u(80)$	$PH_u(80)$	$DS_u(50)$	3
t_2^s	2	$DS_u(60)$	$OP_u(60)$	$PH_u(60)$	$DS_u(40)$	2
t_3^s	3	$DS_{uv}(60)$	$OP_{uv}(60)$	$PH_{uv}(60)$	$DS_{uv}(80)$	1
t_4^s	4	$DS_v(50)$	$OP_v(50)$	$PH_v(50)$	$DS_v(40)$	5
t_5^s	5	$DS_{vw}(60)$	$OP_{vw}(60)$	$PH_{vw}(60)$	$DS_{vw}(50)$	4

(c) Encrypted Relation with user-specified Mixed Encrypted Version

	tid	Sal_DS	Sal_OP	Sal_PH	Inv_DS	ShopID
t_1^s	1	$DS_u(80)$	$OP_u(80)$	$PH_u(80)$	$DS_u(50)$	3
t_2^s	2	$DS_u(60)$	$OP_u(60)$	$PH_u(60)$	$DS_u(40)$	2
t_3^s	3	$DS_u(60)DS_v(60)$	$OP_u(60)OP_v(60)$	$PH_u(60)PH_v(60)$	$DS_u(80)DS_v(80)$	1
t_4^s	4	$DS_v(50)$	$OP_v(50)$	$PH_v(50)$	$DS_v(40)$	5
t_5^s	5	$DS_v(60)DS_w(60)$	$OP_v(60)OP_w(60)$	$PH_v(60)PH_w(60)$	$DS_v(50)DS_w(50)$	4

2.3   An Outsourced Database Example

Considering an original relation R with an access control list (ACL) demonstrated in Table 1(a), three users, u, v, and w, are associated with this table, and the encryption granularity is in attributes. Suppose that the attributes Sales and Inventory must be kept privacy and the ShopID can be in plain, and the following four SQL queries are needed to execute over the relation R.

  q_1: **select** ShopID **from** R **where** Sales $= 60$
  q_2: **select** ShopID **from** R **where** Sales < 65
  q_3: **select** **sum**(Sales) **from** R
  q_4: **select** ShopID **from** R **where** Inventory $= 60$

We consider that the query indexes are directly on encrypted attributes. To perform above queries effectively and efficiently over encrypted data, we need three encryption methods, DS, OP, and PH to encrypt the attribute Sales and Inventory. For example, the comparison and summation are performed on attribute Sales, and it needs the three encryption methods to encrypt the Sales values, respectively. Note that we also need to define four extra attributes, Sal_DS, Sal_OP, Sal_PH, and Inv_DS, to support queries on server side. To simplify the key management at client side for users, the data owner will encrypt all attributes of a tuple with a same key although the attributes and the encryption methods are both different.

An intuitive key assignment method is ACL-specified which means that the encryption key is assigned on the ACL items. For the case in Table 1(a), the key used to encrypt attributes, such as Sales and Inventory, in each tuple depends on the corresponding ACL items. As shown in Table 1(b), these keys are associated with the ACL items. For example, when using the DS encryption method, t_1.Sales, whose value is 80, is encrypted by the key assigned to user u, and the encrypted value is denoted by $DS_u(80)$, while the t_3.Sales, whose value is 60, is encrypted by the key assigned to both user u and user v, and the encrypted value is denoted by $DS_{uv}(60)$.

It is not easy for a specified user to make clear that which ACL item is bound to a certain tuple he can access. To find out the real item in a set of possible ACL item combinations associated with this user, he needs to maintain encryption keys for every possible combination. For a database system with large number of users, it may introduce overloads for database users. For example, when user u issues the query q_1, the condition Sales $= 60$ will be translated into Sal_DS $= DS_u(60)$ **or** Sal_DS $= DS_{uv}(60)$ **or** Sal_DS $= DS_{uw}(60)$ **or** Sal_DS $= DS_{uvw}(60)$. We general it as an OR-expression, OR $\{DS_u(60), DS_{uv}(60), DS_{uw}(60), DS_{uvw}(60)\}$, and this OR-expression is with length 4. In general, when translating a plain query into an encrypted version, the where condition will be translated into an OR-expression. The number of operands in an OR-expression is called as the length of this OR-expression. For the ACL-specified key assignments, the length of OR-expression for n users can be reached to $\sum_{i=0}^{n-1} P_{n-1}^i$ where the notation P_{n-1}^i denotes the number of i-combinations from a set with $n-1$ elements. The ACL-specified key assignment method obviously increases computation costs either in client side or in server side.

We consider the user-specified key assignment method. It means that the data owner will assign each user a key to encrypt the attribute values. Table 1(c) demonstrates the encrypted relation with user-specified key assignments. In this case, the query q_1 issued from user u, the condition Sales = 60 will be translated into Sal_DS = OR $\{DS_u(60)\}$. This makes the size of corresponding OR-expression reach to 1. It is obviously concise and efficient when comparing to the scenario of ACL-specified key assignment.

It seems perfect when executing query over encrypted data with user-specified mixed encryption methods. However, the service provider is a pure storage service provider, he has no obligation to design appropriate storage constraints to separate tuple sets on access rights. A set of encrypted tuples may be leaked intentionally or unintentionally. This means that an adversary user could potentially get some encrypted tuples that he cannot access. Though the adversary cannot take the plain values by decryption, the same encrypted values could open a door to draw inferences on those tuples and thus the inference attack could be launched.

There are two kinds of inferences which could be launched in the Table 1(c).

- *The Intra-attribute-based Inference*   Considering the tuples t_2^s and t_3^s, user u can access t_2^s and t_3^s, and user v can only access t_3^s according to the *ACL* lists. However, v can realize that the decrypted value of t_2^s.Sal_DS is 60 because he finds that the value of t_2^s.Sal_DS is appeared in t_3^s.Sal_DS and he knows that t_3.Sales is 60. Note that in this case, v neither has the right to access t_2 nor has the key associated with user u.
- *The Inter-attribute-based Inference*   Considering the tuples t_4^s and t_5^s, user v can access t_4^s and t_5^s, and user w can only access t_5^s according to the *ACL* lists. However, w can realize that the decrypted value of t_4^s.Sal_DS is 50 because he finds that the value of t_4^s.Sal_DS is appeared in t_5^s.Inv_DS and he knows that t_5.Inventory is 50. Note that in this case, w neither has the right to access t_4 nor has the key associated with user v.

The reason why these attacks could be launched is because of the conflicts introduced by the inconsistent relationships between the equal encrypted attribute values and the unequal access control lists in some tuples. For example, the tuples t_2 and t_3 are such tuples that are conflicting over attribute Sales. This inference can be prevented if the equality relation between encrypted values is destroyed.

3   The Inference Attacks and Defences

In this section, we will explore the inference attack which is based on the equality relations among encrypted attribute values.

We assume that t_i and t_j are two tuples in relation R with N tuples where $t_i \neq t_j$, and $\mathcal{A}$ be the attribute set in R.

3.1 The Intra-attribute Based and Inter-attribute Based Inferences

Definition 1. *The tuples t_i and t_j are called intra-attribute conflicting tuples over attribute A, denoted by $t_i \sim_A t_j$, if the condition, $t_i.A = t_j.A \wedge t_i.ACL \neq t_j.ACL \wedge t_i.ACL \cap t_j.ACL \neq \phi$, is satisfied.*

The notion of conflicting tuple is first proposed in [15]. It describes the conflicts introduced by the mismatch between two tuple with a same value in a specified single attribute (intro-attribute) and different but intersected access control lists. For the tuples in Table 1(a), we have $t_2 \sim_{\mathsf{Sales}} t_3$ because of the satisfied condition $t_2.\mathsf{Sales} = t_3.\mathsf{Sales} \wedge t_2.ACL \neq t_3.ACL \wedge t_2.ACL \cap t_3.ACL \neq \phi$. It means that t_2 and t_3 are intra-attribute conflicting over attribute Sales.

Definition 2. *The tuples t_i and t_j are called inter-attribute conflicting tuples over attributes A and B, denoted by $t_i \sim_{A,B} t_j$, if the condition, $t_i.A = t_j.B \wedge t_i.ACL \neq t_j.ACL \wedge t_i.ACL \cap t_j.ACL \neq \phi$, is satisfied.*

For the tuples in Table 1(a), we have $t_4 \sim_{\mathsf{Sales, Inventory}} t_5$. This is because that the condition $t_4.\mathsf{Sales} = t_5.\mathsf{Inventory} \wedge t_4.ACL \neq t_5.ACL \wedge t_4.ACL \cap t_5.ACL \neq \phi$ is satisfied, and we say t_4 and t_5 are inter-attribute conflicting over attributes Sales and Inventory.

Definition 3. *The encryption method enc $: X \rightarrow Y$ is equality-preserved if $\forall x_1, x_2 \in X$ with $x_1 = x_2$, we have $enc(key, x_1) = enc(key, x_2)$ where key is an encryption key.*

For the encryption methods we discussed previously, both DS and OP methods are equality-preserved, but the PH method is not equality-preserved. Furthermore, both DS and OP are also injective.

Back to the two kinds of inference attacks we discussed before, the logic behind them lies in the observation that the fact of two equal images of an equality-preserved injective mapping implies that the corresponding preimages are equal. Recall the case in Table 1(c), if the attribute values are encrypted by an equality-preserved injective function and an adversary user obtains some encrypted tuples he has no rights to access, he could infer some plain attribute values in those tuples via intra-attribute conflicting or inter-attribute conflicting tuples which he is involved.

As inference instances, if user v can obtain encrypted tuples t_2^s in Table 1(c), he can infer that $t_2^s.\mathsf{Sal\_DS}$ is the encrypted version of value 60 because of the intra-conflicting relationship over attribute Sales between t_2 and t_3. Similarly, if user w can obtain encrypted tuples t_4^s in Table 1(c), he can infer that $t_4^s.\mathsf{Sal\_DS}$ is the encrypted version of value 50 because of the inter-conflicting relationship over attributes Sales and Inventory between t_4 and t_5.

Definition 4. *A function f is conflict-free over $\mathcal{A}$ if $\forall t_i, t_j \in R$ and $\forall A, B \in \mathcal{A}$, $A \neq B$,*

1. *if $t_i \sim_A t_j, \forall u \in t_i.ACL \cap t_j.ACL, f(t_i.A) \neq f(t_j.A)$;*
2. *if $t_i \sim_{A,B} t_j, \forall u \in t_i.ACL \cap t_j.ACL, f(t_i.A) \neq f(t_j.B)$.*

To illustrate the notion of conflict-free function, we consider the two encryption methods, OP and PH, we discussed before. Review the encrypted tuples t_2^s and t_3^s in Table 1(c), user v can access the tuple t_3 but cannot access t_2. He can infer that $t_2.Sales = 60$ by simply comparing the two encrypted values, $t_2^s.Sal\_DS$ and $t_3^s.Sal\_DS$. This is because that user u use DS method to encrypt $t_2.Sales$ and $t_3.Sales$ with the same key. It implies that when the DS method is executed with a same key, it is not conflict-free. Meanwhile, user v cannot infer that $t_2.Sales = 60$ by comparing the two encrypted values, $t_2^s.Sal\_PH$ and $t_3^s.Sal\_PH$. This is because that the PH is executed with a random nonce. Though user u use PH method to encrypt $t_2.Sales$ and $t_3.Sales$ with the same key, the encrypted results stored in $t_2^s.Sal\_PH$ and $t_3^s.Sal\_PH$ are significantly different. It implies that the PH is conflict-free.

We can find that if the encryption function is conflict-free, both inferences could be blocked. The problem is that some encryption functions are equality-preserved if using invariable encryption keys. Changing the encryption keys when encountering conflicting tuples is a possible method to mitigate the inferences. To construct a conflict-free function, we intend to change the equality-preserved function into a kind of piecewise function to destroy the characteristics of equality-preserved in conflicting tuples.

3.2   Constructing Conflict-Free Partitions

Definition 5. *A conflict-free partition $\mathcal{P_A}$ with size m is a set of non-empty tuple sets $\{P_1, P_2, ..., P_m\}$ such that $\cup_{i=1}^{m} P_i = R$, $P_i \cap P_j = \phi$ where $i \neq j$ and $1 \leq i, j \leq m$, and $\forall P \in \mathcal{P_A}, |P| > 1 : \forall t_{i'}, t_{j'} \in P, t_{i'} \neq t_{j'} : \forall A, B \in \mathcal{A}, t_{i'} \nsim_A t_{j'} \wedge t_{i'} \nsim_{A,B} t_{j'}.$*

Considering the last condition in Definition 5, if only the $t_{i'} \nsim_A t_{j'}$ is satisfied, the partition $\mathcal{P_A}$ is called intra-attribute conflict-free, meanwhile, while if only the $t_{i'} \nsim_{A,B} t_{j'}$ is satisfied, the partition $\mathcal{P_A}$ is called inter-attribute conflict-free.

According to the Definition 5, the tuples in the same tuple set P, $P \in \mathcal{P_A}$, are not conflicting tuples. Particularly, if there are N tuples in relation R and we can construct a partition $\mathcal{P_A}$ with size N where each tuple set P_i just contains one tuple. For this case, we say that this conflict-free partition reaches maximum size. Note that when the equality-preserved encryption method is used to encrypt attribute values, a user can use different keys to perform encryption according to the tuple sets in the constructed conflict-free partition and hence makes the encryption method conflict-free. This implies that the size of $\mathcal{P_A}$ determines the number of keys maintained by users. We are interested in finding conflict-free partition with minimum size.

We first consider the graph coloring problems (GCPs). The GCPs are typical NP-hard problems. One of the GCPs is as follows: given an undirected graph $G = (V, E)$ where V is a set of vertices and E is a set of pairs of vertices called edges, and a set of enough number of available colors $S = \{1, 2, ..., k\}$. The problem is to find a minimum number of colors to color the graph such that $u.color \neq v.color$ where $u, v \in V$ and $(u, v) \in E$.

Lemma 1. [15] *Finding an intra-attribute conflict-free partition with minimum size is NP-hard.*

Proof. We only need to translate the problem into a GCP. To construct an undirected graph $G = (V, E)$, translate each tuple t in R into a vertex v and construct E, the set of vertices. For each tuple pair (t_i, t_j), i.e., the corresponding vertex pair (v_i, v_j), add (v_i, v_j) into E, the set of edges, if t_i, t_j are intra-attribute conflicting tuples over attribute A, i.e., $t_i \sim_A t_j$. Considering that the conflict-free partition requires $t_i \nsim_A t_j$ for tuples t_i, t_j in the same partition, it implies that v_i, v_j should have different colors when $(v_i, v_j) \in E$. Therefore finding an intra-attribute conflict-free partition over attribute A with minimum size represent finding a solution for a GCP.

Definition 6. *Let $\mathcal{A} = \{A_1, A_2, ..., A_n\}$, an extended attribute ExtA over $\mathcal{A}$ is the attribute vector $(A_{i_1}, A_{i_2}, ..., A_{i_k})$ where $1 \leq i_1 < i_2 < ... < i_k \leq n$.*

For the example in Table 1(a), let $\mathcal{A} = \{$Sales, Inventory, ShopID$\}$. The extended attribute SI can be defined as SI = (Sales, Inventory).

Definition 7. *Let t_i and t_j be two tuples in relation R over $\mathcal{A} = \{A_1, A_2, ..., A_n\}$ and ExtA is an extended attributes over $\mathcal{A}$, $t_i.ExtA =_{ext} t_j.ExtA$ if $\exists k : 1 \leq k \leq n : t_i.A_k = t_j.A_k \vee \exists k_1, k_2 : 1 \leq k_1 < k_2 \leq n, t_i.A_{k_1} = t_j.A_{k_2}$.*

Following the example previously, as the extended attribute SI is introduced, we have $t_2.SI =_{ext} t_3.SI$ because of $t_2.$Sales $= t_3.$Sales. And also $t_4.$Sales $= t_5.$Inventory because of $t_4.SI =_{ext} t_5.SI$.

Definition 8. *The tuples t_i and t_j are called conflicting tuples over the extended attribute ExtA, denoted by $t_i \sim_{ExtA} t_j$, if the condition, $t_i.ExtA =_{ext} t_j.ExtA \wedge t_i.ACL \neq t_j.ACL \wedge t_i.ACL \cap t_j.ACL \neq \phi$, is satisfied.*

Considering the ACL relationships among tuples t_2, t_3, t_4, and t_5, it is easy to show that $t_2 \sim_{SI} t_3$ and $t_4 \sim_{SI} t_5$.

In general, the conflict-free partition over attribute set $\mathcal{A}$ can be viewed as the intra-attribute conflict-free partition over attribute extA, we have the following lemma.

Lemma 2. *Finding a conflict-free partition is equivalent to finding an intra-attribute conflict free partition over an extended attribute.*

Proof. Let ExtA be an extended attribute over $\mathcal{A} = \{A_1, A_2, ..., A_n\}$. For two conflicting tuples t_i and t_j over ExtA, the notation $t_i \sim_{ExtA} t_j$ implies that $t_i.ExtA =_{ext} t_j.ExtA$, i.e., $\exists k : 1 \leq k \leq n : t_i.A_k = t_j.A_k \vee \exists k_1, k_2 : 1 \leq k_1 < k_2 \leq n, t_i.A_{k_1} = t_j.A_{k_2}$, and $t_i.ACL \neq t_j.ACL \wedge t_i.ACL \cap t_j.ACL \neq \phi$. It also implies that t_i and t_j are intra-attribute conflicting tuples over a certain attribute or inter-attribute conflicting tuples over two attributes. According to the Definition 5, the conflict-free partition $\mathcal{P}_{ExtA}$ is also the conflict-free partition $\mathcal{P}_{\mathcal{A}}$, and we have the conclusion.

With previously discussed two lemmas, we have the following theorem.

Theorem 1. *Finding a conflict-free partition with minimum size is NP-hard.*

Proof. According to Lemma 2, finding a conflict-free partition over $\mathcal{A}$ is equivalent to finding an intra-attribute conflict free partition over an extended attribute ExtA. According to Lemma 1, finding an intra-attribute conflict-free partition with minimum size is NP-hard. Therefore, finding a conflict-free partition with minimum size is NP-hard.

3.3   The Algorithms

If we can find a conflict-free partition and define a conflict-free function over tuple sets according to the conflict-free partition, we can find a solution to prevent the inference attacks. A simple and direct strategy is combining random salts with user-specified keys when encrypting data attributes. If two tuples in a same partition are accessible to user u, the same salt can be used to construct a key and then encrypt attribute values in both tuples, i.e., the encryption key is the same when user u performs attribute encryptions on the two tuples. Meanwhile, if two tuples in different partitions, the corresponding salts are different. It means that different keys are used by user u when he encrypts tuples in different partitions. The number of salts depends on the size of partition.

However, as described in Theorem 1, finding a conflict-free partition with minimum size is NP-hard. It needs heuristic methods to find approximate optimal solutions. There are two ways to construct a conflict-free partition. The attribute level method defines partitions on each single attribute while the relation level method defines partitions on a set of attributes. The attribute level method may introduce smaller sizes of conflict-free partitions but may also lead to intricate computations. For example, it needs to determine the number of salts for each attributes. Considering that we will perform analytical computations on encrypted data, the relation level method is a better choice. We will adopt a relation level heuristic method. Algorithm 1 demonstrates such a method to find conflict-free partition $\mathcal{P}_\mathcal{A}$ over attribute set $\mathcal{A}$.

According to this algorithm, we initialize the conflict-free partition $P_\mathcal{A}$ as an empty set. When given a tuple t, we will distribute it into a chosen partition $P \in P_\mathcal{A}$ such that t does not conflict with any tuples in P. To achieve this, we first construct a set of candidate partitions $CandP$ where each partition $P \in CandP$ is the possible partition that t will be distributed. If the set $CandP$ is empty, we create a new partition, distribute t into it, and append it into $P_\mathcal{A}$. Otherwise, we random choose a partition $P \in CandP$ and distribute t into P. This procedure will be continued until all tuples are distributed, and finally, we can obtain a conflict-free partition $P_\mathcal{A}$.

We use the notation $t.u.salt$ to represent the salt that user u used in tuple t. The process of salt assignment is demonstrated in Algorithm 2.

As shown in Algorithm 2, we use the conflict-free partition constructed by Algorithm 1 to assign salts user by user. For each user u and each partition $C \in P_\mathcal{A}$, we extract tuple set $P_u, P_u \subseteq C$, where u is accessible to each tuple in P_u. We assign a salt $salt_u$ to u to construct a key to encrypt attributes in

Algorithm 1. Constructing Conflict-free Partition $\mathcal{P}_\mathcal{A}$ over Attribute Set $\mathcal{A}$

1: $\mathcal{P}_\mathcal{A} = \phi$
2: **for** each $t \in R_\mathcal{A}$ **do**
3:   **if** $\mathcal{P}_\mathcal{A} == \phi$ **then**
4:     $P = \{t\}$
5:     $\mathcal{P}_\mathcal{A} = \mathcal{P}_\mathcal{A} \cup \{P\}$
6:   **else**
7:     $CandP = \{P | P \in \mathcal{P}_\mathcal{A} : \forall t' \in P : \forall \mathsf{A}, \mathsf{B} \in \mathcal{A} : t' \nsim_\mathsf{A} t \wedge t' \nsim_{\mathsf{A},\mathsf{B}} t\}$
8:     **if** $CandP \neq \phi$ **then**
9:       random pick $P_r \in CandP$
10:      $P_r = P_r \cup \{t\}$
11:    **else**
12:      $P = \{t\}$
13:      $\mathcal{P}_\mathcal{A} = \mathcal{P}_\mathcal{A} \cup \{P\}$
14:    **end if**
15: **end if**
16: **end for.**

$t \in P_u$. Hence, user u can build a private index with private selected random salt for mixed encrypted databases over encrypted data.

Algorithm 2. Assigning *salt* via the Conflict-free Partition $\mathcal{P}_\mathcal{A}$

1: **for** each user u **do**
2:   $i = 1$
3:   **for** each $P \in \mathcal{P}_\mathcal{A}$ **do**
4:     $P_u = \{t | t \in P \wedge u \in t.ACL\}$
5:     **if** $P_u \neq \phi$ **then**
6:       $salt_u = GenerateSalt_u(i)$
7:       **for** each $t \in P_u$ **do**
8:         $t.u.salt = salt_u$
9:       **end for**
10:      $i = i + 1$
11:    **end if**
12: **end for**
13: **end for.**

4   Extra Attributes for Supporting SQL Queries

4.1   Representation of Set Data

With the user-specified mixed encryption, multiple encrypted values (one for each authorized user and the number is associated to the user number in corresponding ACL item) may be defined for the same encrypted attribute. Formally, a tuple t with access control item ACL will be firstly translated into a tuple set $T_t = \{t_u | t_u = t \wedge u \in t.ACL \wedge t_u.ACL = \{u\}\}$, and then user $u \in t.ACL$ will encrypt t_u combining with assigned salt. The multiple encrypted values means that the attribute is a set type. However, current SQL database implementations do not support this kind of attribute. We will adopt the duplicating-tid strategy to support the representation of sets of values. As an example, after finishing the process of conflict-free partition and the salt assignment, the table in Table 1(c) is translated into the table in Table 2.

As an example for encrypted attributes in Table 2, we analyze the notation $DS_u(u_1, 80)$ for attribute Sal_DS. This notation denotes an encrypted value of 80. Firstly, user u combine salt u_1 with the secret shared with the data owner to generate a private key. And then, this key is used in DS encryption to encrypt the value 80. Finally, the encrypted value is obtained and denoted by $DS_u(u_1, 80)$. Other encrypted attributes can be analyzed in similar way except the attribute Sal_PH. As an example, the notation $PH_u(80)$ denotes the value 80 is encrypted with a PH method and the encryption key is from the secret shared between user u and the data owner.

To support SQL query over encrypted data on our proposed indexes, we add two attributes, the attribute tid is used to distinguish the duplicate tuples in original tables and the attribute sid is used to represent the salt used in this tuple. We use user-specified function $sid()$ to generate corresponding sid values. For example, we can define $sid()$ by using a cryptological hash function.

Table 2. Conflict-free encrypted relation with mixed encrypted relation.

tid	sid	Sal_DS	Sal_OP	Sal_PH	Inv_DS	ShopID
1	$sid_u(u_1)$	$DS_u(u_1, 80)$	$OP_u(u_1, 80)$	$PH_u(80)$	$DS_u(u_1, 50)$	3
2	$sid_u(u_1)$	$DS_u(u_1, 60)$	$OP_u(u_1, 60)$	$PH_u(60)$	$DS_u(u_1, 40)$	2
3	$sid_u(u_2)$	$DS_u(u_2, 60)$	$OP_u(u_2, 60)$	$PH_u(60)$	$DS_u(u_2, 80)$	1
3	$sid_v(v_1)$	$DS_v(v_1, 60)$	$OP_v(v_1, 60)$	$PH_v(60)$	$DS_v(v_1, 80)$	1
4	$sid_v(v_1)$	$DS_v(v_1, 50)$	$OP_v(v_1, 50)$	$PH_v(50)$	$DS_v(v_1, 40)$	5
5	$sid_v(v_2)$	$DS_v(v_2, 60)$	$OP_v(v_2, 60)$	$PH_v(60)$	$DS_v(v_2, 50)$	4
5	$sid_w(w_1)$	$DS_w(w_1, 60)$	$OP_w(w_1, 60)$	$PH_w(60)$	$DS_w(w_1, 50)$	4

To support the SQL queries over the proposed conflict-free mixed encrypted database, each user u has the knowledge of: (1)the maximum number of random salts for tuples that he can access; (2)the salt generation function used by the data owner to generate; (3)the secret shared by the data owner to construct encryption key.

4.2   Examples of Query Translation

Recall the queries we discussed in Sect. 2

q_1: **select** ShopID **from** R **where** Sales $= 60$

q_2: **select** ShopID **from** R **where** Sales < 65

q_3: **select** **sum**(Sales) **from** R

q_4: **select** ShopID **from** R **where** Inventory $= 60$

We consider the single equality query q_1. The server side query translation for q_1 is direct. When user u issues this query, q_1 will be translated into $q^s_{u,1}$: **select** ShopID **from** R^s **where** Sal_DS $=$ OR $\{DS_u(u_1, 60), DS_u(u_2, 60)\}$. The length of translated OR-expression is not bigger than the maximum salt number for user u encrypting tuples.

It is something different when user a, the *Administrator*, issues this query, it will be translated into $q^s_{a,1}$: **select distinct** ShopID **from** R^s **where** Sal_DS $=$ OR $\{DS_u(u_1, 60), DS_u(u_2, 60), DS_v(v_1, 60), DS_v(v_2, 60), DS_w(w_1, 60)\}$. In this case, the length of translated OR-expression is not bigger than the sum of all the maximum salt number for each users.

Similar methods could be adopted to the query q_4 because it is also a single equality query.

For the query q_2, the introduction of salt destroy the preserved order in attribute Sal_OP for each user, we add an auxiliary attribute, sid, into encrypted relation to distinguished different salts. For example, when user u issues this query, it will be translated into $q^s_{u,2}$: **select** ShopID **from** R^s **where** OR $\{(\text{sid} == sid_u(u_1) \text{ and } \text{Sal\_OP} < OP_u(u_1, 65)), (\text{sid} == sid_u(u_2) \text{ and } \text{Sal\_OP} < OP_u(u_2, 65))\}$.

For the query q_3, the computation is different. The **sum** can be directly computed over encrypted data because of the additive homomorphic encryption. When user u issues this query, the server side query $q^s_{u,3}$ will be as **select** **sum**(Sal_PH) **from** R^s **where** sid $=$ OR $\{sid_u(u_1), sid_u(u_2)\}$. However, when user *Administrator*, the query will be translated into following sequences:

1. **select distinct** tid, sid, Sal_PH **into** $TempR^s$ **from** R^s
2. **select** @$sum_u =$ **sum**(Sal_PH) **from** $TempR^s$ **where** sid $=$ OR $\{sid_u(u_1), sid_u(u_2)\}$
3. **select** @$sum_v =$ **sum**(Sal_PH) **from** $TempR^s$ **where** sid $=$ OR $\{sid_v(v_1), sid_v(v_2)\}$
4. **select** @$sum_w =$ **sum**(Sal_PH) **from** $TempR^s$ **where** sid $=$ OR $\{sid_w(w_1)\}$
5. @$sum = sum_u + sum_v + sum_w$

5   Some Considerations in Managing Encrypted Tuples

Algorithms 1 and 2 are used to initialize the conflict-free encrypted database when translating a plain one. However, data tuples are not always in static, the operations, such as insert and delete, may make tuples dynamic. It is important to keep data tuples conflict-free after the dynamic operations.

5.1   Conflicting Tuples with Respect to Injective Functions

Definition 9. *The tuples t_i and t_j are called intra-attribute conflicting tuples with respect to function f over attribute A, denoted by $f(t_i) \sim_A f(t_j)$, if the condition, $f(t_i.A) = f(t_j.A) \wedge t_i.ACL \neq t_j.ACL \wedge t_i.ACL \cap t_j.ACL \neq \phi$, is satisfied.*

For example, tuple t_2 and tuple t_3 in Table 1(a) are intra-attribute conflicting tuples with respect to encryption function DS over attribute Sales when user u encrypts attribute Sales values in these two tuples with the same encryption key.

Definition 10. *The tuples t_i and t_j are called inter-attribute conflicting tuples with respect to function f over attributes A and B, denoted by $f(t_i) \sim_{A,B} f(t_j)$, if the condition, $f(t_i.A) = f(t_j.B) \wedge t_i.ACL \neq t_j.ACL \wedge t_i.ACL \cap t_j.ACL \neq \phi$, is satisfied.*

For example, tuple t_4 and tuple t_5 in Table 1(a) are inter-attribute conflicting tuples with respect to encryption function DS over attribute Sales and attribute Inventory when user v encrypts attribute Sales value in t_4 and attribute Inventory value in t_5 with the same encryption key.

Theorem 2. *Given an injective function f, A, B are attributes, and two tuples t_i and t_j are over relation R,*

(1). if $f(t_i) \sim_A f(t_j)$, $t_i \sim_A t_j$;
(2). if $f(t_i) \sim_{A,B} f(t_j)$, $t_i \sim_{A,B} t_j$.

Proof. Since f is an injection, we have $t_i.A = t_j.A$ because of $f(t_i.A) = f(t_j.A)$. Considering that $t_i.ACL \neq t_j.ACL \wedge t_i.ACL \cap t_j.ACL \neq \phi$, we have $t_i \sim_A t_j$. Similarly, we have $t_i \sim_{A,B} t_j$ if $f(t_i) \sim_{A,B} f(t_j)$.

With Theorem 2 and considering that the DS and OP encryption methods are injective, we can perform both inter- and intra-attribute-based conflict tests over encrypted tuples at server side.

We define a server-running test function $\mathsf{IsConflicted}_u(f(s, t^*))$ to test whether or not there exists a conflicting tuple with respect to f over a certain attribute or attribute pair for a tuple t^*, where f where s is a salt maintained by user u. The function $\mathsf{IsConflicted}_u(f(s, t^*))$ returns TRUE if there exists a tuple t such that t and t^* are intra- or inter-attribute conflicting tuples with respect to function f, that is, $\exists A, B \in \mathcal{A}, t \in R, u \in t^*.ACL \cap t.ACL : f(s, t^*) \sim_A f(s, t) \vee f(s, t^*) \sim_{A,B} f(s, t)$, otherwise, returns FALSE.

We also define two sets for storing sid data for user u, while the set SID_u is for currently using and the set $RSID_u$ is for revoked *sids*.

5.2   Delete an Encrypted Tuple

Removing an existing tuple cannot introduce any conflicting tuples, our attention is in managing salt identifier *sid* related to some users. For user u, If salt identifier sid_u of the deleting tuple does not appear in encrypted database after deletion, we will put it into the revoked salts set $RSID_u$. Algorithm 3 sketches the procedure of deleting a tuple from an encrypted table.

Algorithm 3. Delete an encrypted tuple rt

1: **for** each $u \in rt.ACL$ **do**
2:     $RSid_u = \{t | t \in R \wedge u \in t.ACL \wedge t.sid == rt.sid_u\}$
3:     **if** $|RSid_u| == 1$ **then**
4:         Insert $rt.sid_u$ into $RSID_u$
5:         Remove $rt.sid_u$ from SID_u
6:     **end if**
7:     Delete rt_u
8: **end for**.

5.3   Insert a New Tuple

When inserting a new tuple into the encrypted relation, a key issue is to choose a specified salt to make the tuple conflict-free with each other. To reduce the salt number that a user maintains, the first choice is to reuse the salt from the salt set currently using, and then considering a revoked one which was used ever, and finally use a new generating one.

Algorithm 4 sketches the procedure of insertion. We use *status* denote the three sources that the salt s comes from, while SID_SALT denotes from currently using salts, RSID_SALT from revoked salts, and NEW_SALT a new generated salt. To reuse one of the currently using salts, it is important to avoid conflicts when using this salt in encryption. For each encryption method addressed in attribute value encryption (in our case, the DS and OP), the encrypted value must pass the conflict test IsConflicted($\cdot$) to ensure the inserted tuple conflict-free. For the salt comes from revoked salts, the corresponding *sid* must be removed from the revoked *sid* set $RSID$ and insert into the currently using set SID. Also, if the salt is the new generated salt, its *sid* must be inserted into SID.

5.4   Update a Tuple

Updating a tuple will change some attribute values and hence may introduce new coming conflicting. A simple strategy to perform update operation is delete-insert. This implies that deleting a tuple at first and insert a new tuple with an updated one.

6   Defending Against Frequency-Based Linking Attack

As we discussed before, some encryption methods, such as DS and OP, are equality-preserved, it also implies that the frequencies of encrypted data are related to the ones of original plain values. When an adversary user has some background knowledge, such as some original value distributions, the frequency-based linking attacks could be launched. It is useful to mitigate the equality relations between plain values and encrypted values. We consider a defence method to protect the encrypted value distribution based on information theory.

Algorithm 4. Insert new tuple nt

1: **for** each $u \in nt.ACL$ **do**
2:     $status = \text{NOT\_CHOOSEN}$
3:     **repeat**
4:         random select $sid \in SID_u$
5:         find salt s such that $sid(s) == sid$
6:         **if** ($\forall$ Encryption method enc: $\text{IsConflicted}_u(enc(s, nt)) == \text{FALSE}$) **then**
7:             $tsalt = s$
8:             $status = \text{SID\_SALT}$
9:             **break**
10:         **end if**
11:     **until** SID_u has been traversed
12:     **if** $status == \text{NOT\_CHOOSEN}$ **then**
13:         **repeat**
14:             random select $sid \in RSID_u$
15:             find salt s such that $sid_u(s) == sid$
16:             **if** ($\forall$ Encryption method enc:$\text{IsConflicted}_u(enc(s, nt)) == \text{FALSE}$) **then**
17:                 $tsalt = s$
18:                 $status = \text{RSID\_SALT}$
19:                 Insert $sid_u(tsalt)$ into SID_u
20:                 Remove $sid_u(tsalt)$ from $RSID_u$
21:                 **break**
22:             **end if**
23:         **until** $RSID_u$ has been traversed
24:     **end if**
25:     **if** $status == \text{NOT\_CHOOSEN}$ **then**
26:         generate a new salt $tsalt$
27:         Insert $sid_u(tsalt)$ into SID_u
28:         $status = \text{NEW\_SALT}$
29:     **end if**
30:     $nt_u \leftarrow$ Encrypted nt with salt $tsalt$
31:     Insert nt_u into R
32: **end for.**

6.1   Information Entropy

The concept of entropy is the central role of information theory. The entropy of a random variable is defined in terms of its probability distribution and can be shown to be a good measure of randomness or uncertainty.

Let the ensemble X be a triple (x, D_x, P_x), where the outcome x is the value of a random variable, the set $A_x = \{a_1, a_2, ..., a_n\}$ is a set of possible values, the set $P_x = \{p_1, p_2, ..., p_n\}$ is a set of probabilities with $p(x = a_i) = p_i, p_i \geq 0$ and $\sum_{a_i \in A_x} p_i = 1$. Assume that $0 \cdot \log 0 = 0$, the entropy of the ensemble X can be defined by

$$H(X) = - \sum_{x \in A_x} p(x) \cdot \log p(x),$$

which measures the average information content or uncertainty of the ensemble X.

Recall the case of encrypted data, let EV be the encrypted value set when using an equality-preserved encryption method enc, $EV = \{e | e = \langle v, ev, n_e \rangle \wedge ev = enc(v)\}$ with v is an attribute value and n_e is the frequency of ev appeared in encrypted database. Let $N = \sum_{ev} n_e$, the following formula can be used to compute the entropy of EV:

$$H(EV) = - \sum_e \frac{n_e}{N} \cdot \log \frac{n_e}{N}$$

We use the above formula to measure the degree of original data distribution protected in a given encrypted database. It is obviously that the $H(EV)$ reaches its maximize value $\log |EV|$ when the frequencies of each encrypted value are the same.

6.2 The Defence Method

Intuitively if the frequencies of each encrypted value are nearly the same, an adversary need more efforts to guess the distribution of encrypted values stored on the database server, even if he knows the probability distribution of original data and a few exact values. This intuition is consistent with the notion of information entropy. It is noted that the information entropy is a measure of unpredictability. The larger the entropy, the more distribution privacy protected in an encrypted database.

Definition 11. *For an element $e = \langle v, ev, n_{ev} \rangle \in EV$, we say e is split into two elements $e_1 = \langle v, ev_1, n_{e_1} \rangle$, $e_2 = \langle v, ev_2, n_{e_2} \rangle$ iff all the original value v are encrypted into two different values ev_1 and ev_2, and $n_{e_1} \neq 0, n_{e_2} \neq 0$.*

We denote EV_s as the new encrypted value set after an element is split. This leads $EV_s = EV \cup \{e_1, e_2\} - \{e\}$.

Theorem 3. *If an element $e \in EV$ is split into two elements e_1, e_2, we have $H(EV_s) > H(EV)$.*

Proof. We only need to proof that $\frac{n_{e_1} + n_{e_2}}{N} \cdot \log \frac{n_{e_1} + n_{e_2}}{N} > \sum_{i=1}^{2} \frac{n_{e_i}}{N} \cdot \log \frac{n_{e_i}}{N}$. Since $n_{e_1} \neq 0, n_{e_2} \neq 0$, we have $\log \frac{n_{e_1} + n_{e_2}}{N} > \log \frac{n_{e_1}}{N}$. And then $\frac{n_{e_1}}{N} \log \frac{n_{e_1} + n_{e_2}}{N} > \frac{n_{e_1}}{N} \log \frac{n_{e_1}}{N}$. Similarly, $\frac{n_{e_2}}{N} \log \frac{n_{e_1} + n_{e_2}}{N} > \frac{n_{e_2}}{N} \log \frac{n_{e_2}}{N}$. And we have the result.

This theorem indicates that when an element is split into two elements, the entropy of encrypted value set becomes larger.

Theorem 4. *If user u performs the split operation over encrypted data, the salt number is increased at most one.*

Proof. Suppose an attribute value *value* is encrypted by user u with salt s and the encrypted data, $DS_u(s, value)$, have n $(n > 1)$ occurrences. Obviously, any encrypted tuples with $DS_u(s, value)$ are not conflicting with other tuples. Suppose n is splitted into two positives, n_1 and n_2, where $n_1 + n_2 = n$. We keep the $DS_u(s, value)$ appears in n_1 occurrences, i.e., use the same salt s encrypt n_1 *values*. For the remaining n_2 *values*, we choose another salt s' to perform encryption as methods described in Algorithm 4 and make $DS_u(s', value)$ be not conflicting with other tuples. In worst case, s' is the new salt, and hence, the salt number is increased at most one.

To defend against frequency-based linking attacks, a simple strategy is to split same attribute values for each user to change the encrypted value frequency distribution. For each user, the introduced cost is at most to manage one more extra salt. Furthermore, we can define a threshold value α such that the entropy of encrypted value after split is at least α.

7   Experiments and Discussion

7.1   Measuring Query Time Cost Based on OR-Expression

The introduction of random salts will make the **where** condition of a plain SQL query translate into an OR-expression. Different lengths of OR-expression may lead to different SQL query response time. We run a set of experiments to confirm this intuition.

These experiments are on an HP mini-210 with Intel Atom N450 1.66 GHz and 1 GB memory, running Windows XP sp3 and MS SQL2000. We create 5 tables with 20k integers where those integers are evenly distributed in intervals $[1, 1k], [1, 2k], [1, 5k], [1, 10k]$, and $[1, 20k]$, respectively, and the 5 tables are denoted by T_i with $i = 1, 2, 3, 4, 5$.

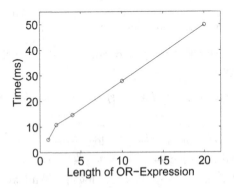

Fig. 2. Time cost on OR-expression

The executed queries are in the defined form **select** $*$ *from T* **where** OR-*expression*. We regulate the OR-expression in order to retrieve 20 tuples on each table. For example, given $a \in [1, 1k]$, the query, **select** $* \, from \, T_1$ **where** $value = a$, will return 20 tuples. While given $a, b \in [1, 1k]$, the query, **select** $* \, from \, T_2$ **where** $value = a$ **or** $alue = b$, will also return 20 tuples. The time cost comparisons in these two queries can be used to demonstrate the query performance comparisons between OR-expressions with length 1 and length 2.

In our conducted experiments, we randomly generate the OR-expression, execute the query, and record the response time. The average time in 1,000 tests is shown as in Fig. 2.

Figure 2 demonstrates that as the length of OR-expression increases, the query retrieved the same number of tuples needs more response times. Considering that the length of OR-expression is associated with number of salts, the number of salts can approximate reflect the query performance of our proposed method.

7.2   Measuring Salt Numbers Users Maintained

To evaluate the behavior of our proposed method, we need two types of materials for experiments, the data tuples and the authorized users for tuples.

For the data tuples, we first generate a relational table with 800000 tuples following the TPC-H benchmark specifications, and then randomly select $3000, 8000, 13000$, and 18000 tuples to construct tables Data3k, Data8k, Data13k, and Data18k, respectively. Each table contain the same three attributes, including $10000, 9999$, and 1000 distinct integers, respectively.

For the authorized users for tuples, we extract the authors coauthored with Professor Xuemin Shen from the DBLP repository. In particular, we extract the top m most productive authors and construct authors set of size n from the repository. We view the constructed authors set as the authorized users set, i.e., the ACL lists for tuples. In our experiments, we set m as 40, 90, 140, and 190, respectively, and correspondingly, we set n as 60, 124, 204, and 297, respectively. We denote our constructed ACL lists as $ACL1$, $ACL2$, $ACL3$, and $ACL4$, respectively.

We construct the conflict-free partitions for each instance table with each constructed ACL list and compute the maximum/median number of salts assigned to each user. We repeat the computation 100 times and compute the average maximum/median number of salts per user. Our experiments are focused on counting the number of salts assigned to users. This is because that the number of salts per user assigned determines the extra computation costs when a user executes SQL queries at client side.

Figure 3 demonstrates the average number of salts per user on different datasets, where Fig. 3(a) shows the average maximum salt number and Fig. 3(b) shows the average median salt number. We find that as the number of tuples increasing, both maximum number and median number are also increasing. For the average maximum number of salts a user could be used is limited in the interval $[4, 12]$. This means that when translating client side SQL queries into server side query versions, the average number of test index values is at most 12. Comparing with the ACL-specified indexes, we can achieve the same query results with much smaller computation overloads in both client side and server side. It is noted that in our experiments, the maximum salt numbers are closely related with the tuple numbers. It is almost irrelevant with the sizes of ACL lists.

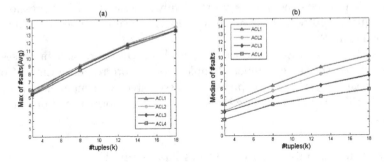

Fig. 3. Average number of salts per user on tuples

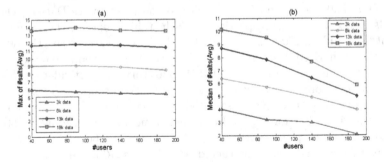

Fig. 4. Average number of salts per user on users

On the other hand, as demonstrated in Fig. 4 with Fig. 4(a) shows the average maximum salt number and Fig. 4(b) shows the average median salt number per user, respectively, comparing to the user numbers. We find that the number of salts is decreased as the number of users is increased when given a certain dataset. This is because the increased number of users will decrease the possibilities of conflicting tuples.

7.3 Related Work

Outsourcing data to third parties out of the control of data owners requires storing data encrypted on remote servers. To avoid storing many different encrypted versions of a same tuple on servers, encrypting each tuple with a single key is a common knowledge. Since the early efforts on outsourced databases [4, 7] are focused on how to translate the client-side plain queries into corresponding server-side encrypted versions, they assume that all the tuples are encrypted by a same key. It implies that a certain user may have the full rights to access any encrypted tuples if he gets the decryption key.

The selective encryption methods use different keys to encrypt different data portions such as tuples or attributes [9]. To avoid users from managing too many keys, the keys can be derived from user hierarchy [5]. And also, the traditional ciphers are replaced with the attribute-based encryption (ABE) method to encrypt data [17]. However, the access controls provided by these methods depend on the readability of decrypted data. This means that some decryption efforts on client side are wasteful.

Other efforts are on developing new ciphers for keyword searching on encrypted data. However, either the symmetric encryption scheme [12] or the asymmetric encryption scheme [16] cannot prevent the curious service provider locating the positions with the same method. We note that locating encrypted tuples implies execute comparison operations over encrypted data on server without decryption. The partially [10] or fully [6] homomorphic encryption methods can be used to perform the comparison. But, as mentioned previously, if the comparison results could be distinguished on server, the curious service provider could also manipulate in the same way to obtain the results of comparison.

To improves the speed of encrypted data retrieval operations on server, several index techniques are proposed. The CryptDB scheme [11] defines layers of encryption for different types of database queries. For executing a specific query, layers of encryption are removed by decrypting to an appropriate layer and the tuple index is directly on the encrypted data. This method may lead many sensitive values be stored to the level defined by the weakest encryption scheme. No inference attacks are considered in this scheme. Based on the CryptDB scheme, MONOMI [14] can support more analytical queries over encrypted data by split query execution across client side and server side. Although both schemes support different keys to encrypt different tuples, they do not consider the inference attacks addressed in our works.

The DAS (Database as a Service) model [7] proposes a bucketization method to construct the index. This index is defined on an auxiliary attribute which is associated with the corresponding original attribute. However, there is no formal security analysis about this kind of index. Value-based index is discussed in [4]. Comparing with the bucketization index, the value-based index locate encrypted data in high accuracy but also disclose many other useful information such as the data distribution. Based on the DAS model, the authors in [8] deeply analyze the bucketization technique and algorithmically build privacy-preserving indexes on sensitive attributes. However, their assumptions are on shared data in users. It implies that all the attribute values are encrypted with a single key and the index tags are built on value intervals.

To our knowledge, the authors in [15] firstly address the inferences of encrypted data in outsourced databases. They discuss a kind of inference attack introduced by the value-based index. The addressed inferences are on the explicit equality relations among tuples with different access rights which we call intra-attribute based inference in this paper. But they do not address the inter-attribute based inference on the equality relations between attributes. In [13], the authors propose secure distributed querying protocols based on the use of secure hardware in client side. They also partition query execution across client side and server side and introduce fake tuples to defend against frequency-based attacks. However, the fake tuples would limit the computation over encrypted data and introduce some more post-decryption efforts to filter those fake tuples.

8   Conclusion

Ensuring data privacy and improving query performance are two closely linked challenges for outsourced databases. Using different encryption methods to data attributes can reach an explicit trade-off between these two challenges. However, encryption cannot always conceal relations between attribute values. When the data tuples are accessed selectively, inference attacks by comparing encrypted values could be launched. In this paper, we explore the intra-attribute based and inter-attribute based inferences in mixed encrypted databases. We develop a method to construct private indexes on user-specified encrypted values to defend against the inferences while supporting efficient selective access to encrypted data. Possible future work may include the data consistency management in various encrypted versions and the defence of inference attacks which is introduced by the collusion between other users and the service providers.

References

1. Agrawal, R., Kiernan, J., Srikant, R., Xu, Y.: Order-preserving encryption for numeric data. In: Proceedings of SIGMOD 2004, pp. 563–574 (2004)
2. Boldyreva, A., Chenette, N., Lee, Y., O'Neill, A.: Order-preserving symmetric encryption. In: Joux, A. (ed.) EUROCRYPT 2009. LNCS, vol. 5479, pp. 224–241. Springer, Heidelberg (2009)
3. Boldyreva, A., Chenette, N., O'Neill, A.: Order-preserving encryption revisited: improved security analysis and alternative solutions. In: Rogaway, P. (ed.) CRYPTO 2011. LNCS, vol. 6841, pp. 578–595. Springer, Heidelberg (2011)
4. Damiani, E., Vimercati, S., Jajodia, S., Paraboschi, S., Samarati, P.: Balancing confidentiality and efficiency in untrusted relational DBMSs. In: Proceedings of ACM CCS 2003, pp. 93–102 (2003)
5. Damiani, E., Vimercati, S., Foresti, S., Jajodia, S., Paraboschi, S., Samarati, P.: Key management for multi-user encrypted databases. In: Proceedings of Storage SS 2005, pp. 74–83 (2005)
6. Gentry, C.: Fully homomorphic encryption using ideal lattices. In: Proceedings of STOC 2009, pp. 169–178 (2009)

7. Hacigumus, H., Iyer, B., Li, C., Mehrotra, S.: Executing SQL over encrypted data in the database-service-provider model. In: Proceedings of ACM SIG-MOD 2002, pp. 216–227 (2002)
8. Hore, B., Mehrotra, S., Tsudik, G.: A privacy-preserving index for range queries. In: Proceedings of VLDB 2004, pp. 223–235 (2004)
9. Miklau, G., Suciu, D.: Controlling access to published data using cryptography. In: Proceedings of VLDB 2003, pp. 898–909 (2003)
10. Paillier, P.: Public-key cryptosystems based on composite degree residuosity classes. In: Stern, J. (ed.) EUROCRYPT 1999. LNCS, vol. 1592, pp. 223–238. Springer, Heidelberg (1999)
11. Popa, R., Redfield, C., Zeldovich, N., Balakrishnan, H.: CryptDB: protecting confidentiality with encrypted query processing. In: Proceedings of SOSP 2001, pp. 85–100 (2011)
12. Song, D., Wagner, D., Perrig, A.: Practical techniques for searches on encrypted data. In: Proceedings of IEEE S&P 2000, pp. 44–55 (2000)
13. To, Q., Nguyen, B., Pucheral, P.: Privacy-preserving query execution using a decentralized architecture and tamper resistant hardware. In: Proceedings of EDBT 2014, pp. 487–198 (2014)
14. Tu, S., Kaashoek, M.F., Madden, S., Zeldovich, N.: Processing analytical queries over encrypted data. In: Proceedings of VLDB 2013 (2013)
15. Vimercati, S., Foresti, S., Jajodia, S., Paraboschi, S., Samarati, P.: Private data indexes for selective access to outsourced data. In: Prodeedings of WPES 2011, pp. 69–80 (2011)
16. Yang, G., Tan, C.H., Huang, Q., Wong, D.S.: Probabilistic public key encryption with equality test. In: Pieprzyk, J. (ed.) CT-RSA 2010. LNCS, vol. 5985, pp. 119–131. Springer, Heidelberg (2010)
17. Yu, S., Wang, C., Ren, K., Lou, W.: Achieving secure, scalable, and fine-grained data access control in cloud computing. In: Proceedings of INFO-COM 2010, pp. 534–542 (2010)

Author Index

Printed in the United States
by Bookmasters

Printed in the United States
By Bookmasters